Island Alliance Church
510 Thompson Creek Road
Stevensville, MD 21666-2508

HURT people hurt PEOPLE

HOPE & HEALING
FOR YOURSELF
AND YOUR RELATIONSHIPS

Sandra D. Wilson, Ph.D.

THOMAS NELSON PUBLISHERS
Nashville

Cartoons on pages 13, 24, 63, 104, 109, 120, 131, and 206 are reprinted
from *Will You Marry Me and Be My Mom?* by Mark Giersch (Deerfield
Beach, Florida: Health Communications, Inc., 1989). Used by permission.
Cartoons on pages 145 and 176 are reprinted from *Less Than Entirely Sanc-
tified* by Doug Hall (Downers Grove, Illinois: InterVarsity Press, 1992).
Used by permission.
The drawing on page 48 is reprinted from *It Will Never Happen to Me* by
Claudia Black (Denver: MAC Publishers, 1989). Used by permission.
The drawings on pages 181 and 228 are by Thomas R. Golden and are used
with his permission. For information about Mr. Golden's creations, contact:
(East Coast) Thomas R. Golden, P.O. Box 18160, Philadelphia, PA 19116;
(West Coast) Colleen J. Doherty, Doherty Enterprises, P.O. Box 1503, Whit-
tier, CA 90609-1503.

Published in Nashville, Tennessee, by Thomas Nelson, Inc.
Unless otherwise noted, Scripture quotations are from the NEW KING
JAMES VERSION of the Bible. Copyright © 1979, 1980, 1982, Thomas
Nelson, Inc., Publishers.
Scripture quotations noted NIV are taken from the HOLY BIBLE, NEW
INTERNATIONAL VERSION ®. Copyright © 1973, 1978, 1984 by Inter-
national Bible Society. Used by permission of Zondervan Bible Publishing
House. All rights reserved.
The "NIV" and "New International Version" trademarks are registered in
the United States Patent and Trademark Office by International Bible Soci-
ety. Use of either trademark requires the permission of International Bible
Society.
Scripture quotations noted NASB are from THE NEW AMERICAN STAN-
DARD BIBLE, Copyright © 1960, 1962, 1963, 1968, 1971, 1972, 1973,
1975, 1977 by The Lockman Foundation and are used by permission.
The names, professions, ages, appearances, and other identifying details of
people in this book have been changed to protect their anonymity.

ISBN 0-8407-7746-9

Printed in the United States of America

2 3 4 5 6 7 - 98 97 96 95 94 93

Acknowledgments and Dedication

Although I wrote every word of this book, many people contributed to it in many ways:

Ron Haynes thought "Wilson's Law of Relationships" merited expansion into a book and said so at Thomas Nelson,

Jane Jones and Curtis Lundgren smoothed the path to that goal, and friends and family prayed and encouraged each step of the way.

Each of you, named and unnamed, has my sincere thanks.

With inexpressible joy and gratitude,
I dedicate this book to the

HEALER OF ALL HURTS, JESUS CHRIST

Contents

Introduction

Every time I select a book topic, I find example after example to illustrate the basic premise. I have several topics in mind now and titles to go with them. For example:

Look Ten Years Younger on a Cheesecake Diet
Find Fabulous Wealth from Old Christmas Bows
Increase Your I.Q. Through Chocolate-Loading

I love chocolate and cheesecake. Like most of you, I'd like to look younger and be smarter. And I already have one of the world's largest collections of old Christmas bows. So I'm all set to face the challenge of sudden wealth.

Alas, outrageous book topics like these aren't what God has been using of late to stir my heart. He's been prodding me toward other subjects. At the moment I'm drowning in a sea of newspaper articles and magazine clippings supporting my premise that *hurt people hurt people*. These clippings are about hurt leaders hurting followers; hurt spouses hurting spouses; hurt parents hurting children who hurt younger children.

In one way or another and to one degree or another, invariably God gives me the opportunity to experience up close and personally the struggles and reality represented by my book titles. In my counseling practice and seminary classes and at conferences, I hear all kinds of stories. The details differ, but the core issue is the same: Hurt people hurt people.

What's more, as much as I regret to report it, I see ample evidence that I am both hurt and hurting. I'm guessing you are reading this book because, at least in some measure, you find a shred or two of similar evidence in your life.

It really is true, isn't it? *Hurt people hurt people*. We all have been hurt by people who all were hurt by other hurt people. In turn, we—as hurt people—all have hurt other people to one degree or another. And on and on it goes!

Admittedly, I stretch the word *hurt* very broadly. I mean that our hurts can include intentional and unintentional, visible and invisible, barely survivable to hardly noticeable, other-perpetrated and self-inflicted, hands-on and hands-off actions and attitudes.

The resulting wounds and injuries we usually identify as physical, sexual, emotional, intellectual, verbal, or spiritual neglect or abuse. Most of this wounding does not leave visible marks. Besides, even when these hurts leave physical signs, bruises soon fade and casts come off eventually. So in both cases, we may have only bloodless wounds and unseen soul-scars.

This description may seem rather melodramatic. And you may question my sweeping characterization of us and our interactions. That's fair. So I'll try to answer some of your major questions in these introductory pages.

First, what do hurt people who hurt people look like? They look like human beings, they're easy to spot. (Remember, central to my premise is that *all* of us are hurting people in either small or great ways.)

Still the hurters' identities might shock us. They may be startlingly young, for example. Crime statistics show that approximately 30 percent of rapes and over 50 percent of child molestations are committed by offenders who are under the age of eighteen.[1] More horrifying is the fact that reports are increasing of *children twelve and under molesting other children.*

Overexposed to deviant sexuality, such as promiscuity, pornography, incest, and sexual violence, these children no longer have the normal curiosity of young children. That is, sexually hurt young people are apt to sexually hurt other young people. And when we couch this children-molesting-children tragedy in the language of hurt people hurt people, we trace the answer to a second important question. What do hurt people do to hurt other people?

When people function in areas of their untended wounds and unhealed hurts, they inevitably wound others about as severely as they were hurt and in the same, or remarkably similar, areas. Of course most of our hurting is relatively mild—something like the way a sunburn feels as compared to third-degree burns. Yet many of us deeply wounded have deeply wounded others.

And who are the others we hurt people are most likely to hurt? Usually, we hurt those nearest and dearest to us. To be sure, virtual strangers may superficially or profoundly wound us by their disrespectful rudeness, by their unprovoked violence, or in some other ways. But our deepest wounds happen at the hands of those we love and those who likely love us.

When we first realize that we are most apt to wound those near and dear to us, this can trigger a serious case of the "if onlys." I've had repeated bouts of this life-crippling malady, believe me. My symptoms include thoughts like: "If only I could have met or seen my biological father, even just once." "If only he had wanted me, instead of trying to abort me." "If only my mom had sought help to improve her relationships with men, so I could have seen what a healthy family looks like." "If only I had learned about the effects on me of my stepfather's alcoholism when I was younger, so I could have been a better wife and mother." "If only . . ." "If only . . ."

Perhaps the most global, transcendent "if only" of all is: If only hurt people did *not* hurt people. But they do. To one degree or another, people always have. They are doing it at this very moment. And *they* are *us*!

Pondering this hurt-people-hurt-people premise can leave us feeling pretty hopeless, can't it? And hopelessness is potentially fatal.

I read recently about an elderly man in Detroit who shot himself after killing his wife. His suicide note said he had been diagnosed with Lyme disease. Guilt-stricken, believing his disease was fatal and he had passed it to his wife, he saw no hope for either of them. He concluded that murder and suicide were the only solution.

How tragic! Lyme disease is not contagious, nor is it fatal. But the man's sense of hopelessness was.

When we hurt, we need hope to believe there really is some help for us to stop hurting or, at least, to hurt less. This book offers hope and help for hurting people.

The first six chapters describe the origins and effects of our unseen hurts. But if we stopped there, we would only hurt more. Chapter Seven turns the corner from recognizing how we became hurting and hurtful people to seeing how we can become healing, helpful people. In Chapters Eight through Fourteen, I'll provide help to change in specific relational areas that have been shaped by our hurt-*full* and self-protective ways. Some of these changes are important in our relationships with God, with ourselves, and with other people, such as our friends, spouses, children, and parents. The last chapter focuses on helping us accept the gift of *hope*-full tomorrows, regardless of what we received in our yesterdays.

As you go through the book, you'll see a dozen drawings. Most are cartoons. Some of them you'll probably find more poignant than funny. A few drawings illustrate scenes from hurtful families. I have two main reasons for "stretching" my writing style by including drawings for the first time.

First we can get accustomed to defending ourselves against printed words. This is true especially when the messages the words convey stir unpleasant, even painful, feelings. Drawings have a way of doing an end-run around our defenses and scoring the truth we need to hear.

Second, throughout the book I'll be encouraging us to grieve honestly our unseen wounds and relational losses. We need to cry, but *we also need to laugh.* Of course we don't laugh *at* addictions, neglect, abuse, or intergenerational hurting. But learning now to laugh through our healing from such pain can be a significant part of our changing processes.

As you read, I hope you will pause, ponder, and pray about the sections that bother you. Many people benefit from keeping a personal journal of memories, thoughts, and feelings as they read a book of this kind. You will not "go crazy" or hurt someone just because you feel strong emotions. So give yourself permission from the start to experience whatever emotions stir as you read.

One more question needs to be considered before we begin. In a way it is the most troubling question of all: *Why* do hurt people hurt people? As strange as it may seem, one part of the answer lies in the life-affirming aspect of our humanness that reflects the nature of our Creator.

God is pro-life! He is so devoted to life, he even specializes in bringing life out of death. Jesus said that he came to bring us life—abundant, eternal life. He was even willing to die so that we could live forever with him.

We all bear the Image of God, although sin shattered that Image, to be sure. This means that we all are pro-life. Now, I am pro-life in the anti-abortion sense. But regardless of your stand on abortion, you are pro *your* life. Therefore, when any of us senses a threat to our existence and well-being, we spontaneously act to protect and preserve our lives. For example, it's normal to run, hide, even disguise our identities if necessary when we believe our lives are threatened. And we usually flinch and automatically move to protect a broken bone or raw physical wound when someone suddenly comes too close.

Similarly, in our sin-broken humanness we normally adopt defensive, self-protective thinking and behavior patterns when we feel emotionally or relationally threatened and wounded. This pattern would be different, no doubt, if we were perfect people.

Perfect people wouldn't hurt other people. Perhaps these perfect people wouldn't even have the capacity to experience physical or emotional pain. But if they did, perfect people would, with perfect wisdom and faith, look to their loving Creator for protection and comfort.

As imperfect, sin-broken people, we are prone to trust in ourselves. And the lifestyles we inevitably and unknowingly choose to make us feel more safe and comfortable just end up bringing us more pain. As a side effect, these lifestyles usually bring pain to others.

We don't stop being human when we start being Christian. Even after we have asked Jesus into our lives, we continue to struggle with the human trait of self-protection that leads us to hurt ourselves and others. And our unseen, emotional scars from wounds inflicted by others don't usually disappear anymore than visible, physical scars do.

So when we Christians experience painful suffering, either emotional or physical, we are not strange spiritual misfits. We are human. And we are not backsliding or faithless if we seek human comfort and counsel when we hurt. Even the apostle Paul wasn't ashamed to admit he suffered physically and emotionally. This is the same Paul who, under the Holy Spirit's guidance, wrote that he could do all things through Christ. He told struggling believers that all their needs would be met in the glorious riches of Christ. (See Phil. 4:13 and 19.) But that timeless truth did not change the fact that Paul was still human, needy, and sometimes lonely and hurting. We see his humanity in 2 Corinthians 7:5–6, where he describes himself as physically exhausted and fearful, while still giving thanks to God "who comforts the downcast." In that particular circumstance, by the way, God chose to use a human representative, Titus, to convey his comfort to Paul.

Our tomb-emptying Savior clearly and repeatedly modeled God's inclusion of human co-laborers in his life-giving purposes. (See 1 Cor. 3:9.) In the eleventh chapter of John's gospel, for example, we see Jesus inviting concerned bystanders to participate in the death-to-life drama by telling them to move the stone from Lazarus' tomb. Then he instructed them to remove the graveclothes from Lazarus' body. In between those two activities, Jesus spoke life into the already decomposing body. Notice that Jesus directed human helpers to do what *they* could, while *he* did what he alone could do.

How sad it is that some churches, and even entire denominations, teach that experiencing personal pain and neediness is a symptom of unconfessed sin or galloping self-centeredness. These people teach that seeking human help and comfort means distrusting the sufficiency of God's power. This kind of all-or-nothing point of view limits God's expressing his all-encompassing care.

I really do believe that, no matter what the question, *Jesus is the answer*! I also believe that Jesus often uses human comforters and helpers as he answers.

I pray that our loving Lord Jesus will use this book as part of his comforting and healing process in your life.

CHAPTER One

The Problem of
Unseen Wounds

"Here are four simple words you'll always remember. I call them *Wilson's Law of Relationships.*"

I have spoken that sentence in scores of conferences and seminars across the country in the past few years, and the audiences' responses are amazingly similar wherever I go. Most people smile or chuckle as they scribble my grandiose title in their notes, then look up expectantly to learn what comes next.

"*Wilson's Law of Relationships says: Hurt people hurt people.*"

Suddenly smiles droop. Chuckles evaporate. An intense hush envelopes the audience as many, with eyes glistening, nod their heads and glance knowingly at companions.

As one of those hurt people who has hurt people, I'll confess that I can relate to their responses. In fact, almost everyone I know identifies with the notion that hurt people hurt people. However, I've noticed a curious phenomenon: Even when we relate to this hurting and hurtful quality in ourselves and others, we usually resist the idea that these hurts result in wounds, most of which are unseen.

Let's face it, we are basically walk-by-sight people who "look on the outward appearance," as I Samuel 16:7 says. We usually fail to notice hemorrhaging hearts and lacerated lives, even our own. *Especially* our own. By minimizing, ignoring, and even denying the existence of what we don't see, we act as if *visible* were a synonym for *genuine*.

Clearly, this is a major problem if I'm correct in my assertion that to some degree we are all hurt people, and *hurt people hurt people*. If the hurts are real, the wounds they inflict are real. Clearly too, there are several problems which make it difficult for many of us to accept the reality of unseen wounds. These problems stem from misbelief, and the first of these misbeliefs directly relates to the word *unseen*.

Problem 1: Believing That Unseen Means Unreal

"No tears unless you're bleeding!"

Those were one father's most memorable words, as his adult daughter recalls, according to a full page ad that ran in a nationally circulated newspaper the week before Father's Day, 1992. Those words also express one of the major problems with unseen wounds—they are *unseen!*

Many of us share this parent's if-I-can't-see-it-it-isn't-real perspective. We doubt the reality of wounds unless someone displays scars from *physical* abuse. Others may accept the presence of unseen wounds if they cause some type of organic malfunction. For example, one lovely Christian woman I know was left permanently sterile when her parents performed a coathanger abortion after she was impregnated by her father. She was fourteen at the time.

We probably don't struggle much accepting the fact that this woman has scar tissue damage in her uterus. Why should we be so surprised that she also has unseen scars and damage in her relational, spiritual, and personal life, or that her sexual wounds deeply wound her husband in their sexual relationship? And why should we be amazed to discover that similar dynamics may be operating in our own lives even when the original wounds and their present expressions are entirely different?

"That's just a cop-out for her self-justifying self-centeredness and sin. Tell her to pray, read her Bible more, and snap out of it!"

This response reflects the thinking of many totally sincere Bible-believing Christians. Most of them would be too polite to say it, but I've encountered many who believe it.

Cop-Out for Sin or Context for Change?

Scripture declares that the primary and supremely devastating injury wounding us all is *spiritual*. And it is self-inflicted. Our original parents set the sorry cycle in motion in Eden by trusting their own wisdom and ways instead of their Creator's, whose image they bore.

God did not remove his image—that is, the invisible rational, emotional, relational, and spiritual aspects of himself which he sovereignly chose to share with mankind. But when the image bearers "fell," every aspect of the image was shattered, virtually beyond recognition.

For example, we see the detrimental, life-changing effects of sin in the fallacies and flaws of our human reasoning. This is the primary reason God tells us to seek wisdom from him rather than leaning on our own or another human's imperfect understanding. (See Proverbs 3:5 and Psalm 118:8, for example.)

This is a key concept, because we accept the reality of damaged human thinking processes even though we cannot actually *see* the injuries, wounds, and over-all sin-related irregularities. We believe they exist because we clearly see their effects. For example, when I "rationally" weigh the facts and "logically" conclude that my ideas are almost always right and my exceedingly bright husband's views are almost always wrong, I suspect that may be evidence of my sin-damaged thinking in all its self-serving glory!

So far, we've examined evidence that sin damages our invisible rational/intellectual natures. But we are more than *just* brains.

Emotional and Relational Natures and Wounds

The Bible vividly paints God the Father's emotional nature expressed most clearly in God the Son.[1] And God is not only rational and emotional, God is relational. We see this in the Triune Godhead—Father, Son, and Holy Spirit. God's emotional and relational characteristics are significant elements in the thoroughly sin-shattered *Imago Dei* we still bear. So why would we expect the reality of our wounds and wounding to be any different in our emotional and relational natures than in our intellectual natures?

I've noticed that many well-meaning Christians deny the reality of human vulnerability to unseen emotional injury and pain. Yet, most of these same folks readily acknowledge human vulnerability to *physical* injury and pain without condemning a sufferer's selfishness or lack of faith in God. If the emotion minimizing and denying approach extended to the physical realm, it would sound something like this.

"Bodies are bothersome and potentially dangerous because they can wound and be wounded. So you should ignore your body, disregard physical pain, and live as if human bodies aren't real."

Clearly, such a statement is unbiblical, unhealthy, and unhelpful advice for someone in physical distress. I believe that holds for situations of emotional distress too.

Some people say that this reasoning attempts to cast emotional struggles in a physical suffering mold to excuse the injured from taking personal responsibility for their choices and their lives. I believe that perspective misses the process involved in recovering from physical injuries. In fact, the rehabilitative care model of physical therapy offers a useful pattern for dealing with unseen inner injuries.

The Physical Therapy Model

When it comes to physical injuries, patients are responsible to actively participate with their physical therapists in the healing process. This is true whether the injuries were caused accidentally or purposely by the patients or by others. Furthermore, patients often receive painful "homework assignments" of stretching and exercise, because their care-givers realize that healing doesn't magically occur in the presence of certain medical personnel within some white-walled setting.

When we acknowledge physical injuries we are not "cop-ping out." We are affirming the truth of "pervasive deprav-ity," i.e., that sin damages *all* aspects of *all* people, our bodies included. What's more, we are still personally responsible for what we do about our injuries. Recognizing the nature and extent of physical wounds provides a helpful context from which to work toward the changes that bring greater whole-ness. Non-physical wounds benefit from the same approach.

As we've seen thus far, the first major problem with unseen wounds relates to a misbelief about the word *unseen,* namely that *unseen* is synonymous with *unreal.* We're about to discover that the second significant problem springs from a belief that adults—especially *Christian* adults, should be "beyond" or "above" all that.

Problem 2: Believing We Shouldn't Be "Woundable"

"If I were really a strong Christian, this wouldn't hurt so much. I just wish I could trust God more."

I've heard those words for years as I have counseled with Christian men and women. These dear people struggled with a panorama of painful experiences, including job loss, be-trayal by a mate, recent recollection of parental sexual abuse, and even the death of a parent, child, or spouse.

Many often added something like, "My folks always told me I was too sensitive," "My husband (or wife) tells me I'm just a cry-baby," or perhaps, "My pastor keeps encouraging me to have more faith." Reframed in "unseen wounds" ter-minology, these statements mean, "No matter how severe the injury, I should not be woundable."

Comments like those remind me of a story I once heard from a friend whose father loved learning about people. During a family vacation, he was fascinated to meet the extraordinarily tall doorman at a famous Hollywood restau-rant. In response to the father's questions, this doorman described the challenges of trying to fit into clothes, beds, under doorways, and into life in general. When my friend's dad asked what was the most difficult part, the doorman's eyes suddenly filled with tears. He bent down, rolled up his trouser legs, and said, "This is," as he uncovered bony lower legs and ankles covered with wildly colored fresh and fading bruises.

In a hushed voice the doorman explained, "You see, most people think I am standing on stilts. So they come over and kick my legs as hard as they can, trying to knock me off. Sometimes a half-dozen are kicking me at once. It's all I can do to hold back my tears and keep smiling because I am always in pain."

Have you ever been "kicked," so to speak, by people who seemed to think you were wooden instead of woundable? Have you ever "kicked" others and then been surprised that the relationships were bruised? Where in the world would intelligent adults get the idea that they, or other human beings, ought to be able to *take everything without feeling anything?*

I believe a large part of the answer is found in what I call *binding shame.*

<u>Binding Shame</u>

Shame is the soul-deep belief that something is horribly and uniquely wrong with me that is not wrong with anybody else in the entire world. If I am bound by shame, I feel hopelessly, disgustingly different and worthless. I mean *literally* worth *less* than other people.[2]

You've probably figured out already that the sense of shame I am describing has little or nothing to do with true moral guilt, or what we could call "biblical shame." Scripture clearly pictures *every single one* of us as utterly ruined by sin. Now, I can't be *more* utterly, and you can't either. God invites all of us equally and lovingly to accept his graciously provided salvation, for from God's perspective, no person or group of persons is worth less than others.

So where did a lot of us—yes, me too—ever get the blatantly unbiblical concept of shame? Somebody lied to us when we were too young to read and understand the Bible for ourselves or to accurately interpret the world around us. Actually, it was probably a whole lot of somebodies who likely believed the lie themselves. (Deceived deceivers are just as dangerous and hurtful—if not more so—as calculated deceivers.)

As I see it, shame is rooted in the lie that human beings *can* and *should* be perfect. And being perfect includes possessing the "take-anything factor," i.e., the ability to endure any circumstance whatsoever without feeling anything but "fine" and without behaving any way except "nice."

" MAYBE A FOOTPRINT WILL WORK."

But because I can't seem to be unfailingly fine and nice, I know I am not perfect. And that means I can't fulfill the "Perfect Baby Contract" written for me at birth. (Like the parents in the cartoon, *mine* got *me* to sign because *their* folks got *them* to sign.)

And because I know I'm not perfect, I view myself as hideously flawed. So when I make a mistake, I don't simply *make* a mistake. When I make a mistake, I believe that proves that I *am* a mistake. That's shame's lie in a nutshell! And that shame-lie significantly shapes the "perceptual grid" through which we filter all our experiences.

When I am bound by shame, it seems to ooze from the nucleus of every cell to contaminate all my perceptions, choices, and relationships. What's more, my "I'm-different-and-worth-*less* perspective" leaves me feeling totally separated and isolated from everyone around me. Naturally, I believe that my only chance to connect with all you perfect people comes by either convincing you that I can fill a need in your life, or by tricking you into thinking that I am perfect too.

I don't really understand *why* or exactly *how* I got so hideously different. I just "know" I've *always* been that way. It's like having an invisible, irreparable birth defect. So, of course, that means there is no chance to change—"that's just the way I am." (How many times have you said that to yourself? Or how many times have you heard that concept spoken as "gospel truth" at a family gathering? For example, "Don't make such a big deal out of Grandma's stiletto tongue or Uncle Jeff's dirty jokes, that's just the way she/he is.")

Now what does binding shame have to do with unseen wounds—more specifically, with the issue of our "woundability?" The answer involves a curious malady I've diagnosed in myself and nearly everyone else I know who struggles with the life-shackling effects of shame. With varying degrees of intensity, we experience inner blindness. You see, shame not only *binds* us. Shame *blinds* us. I know.

My Bout with Binding, Blinding Shame

Jesus said, in Matthew 7:9, that normal fathers would not give stones to their children who asked for bread. But some fathers do. You see, not only was my father out of the family and in a federal prison when I was born, he tried repeatedly to prevent my birth by insisting Mother abort me, and then by trying to induce a miscarriage when she refused. When that failed, he tried several times to kill her (and me) in what were supposed to look like gun-cleaning accidents. To save my mom's life—and mine—God used the federal authorities to track down and imprison my father.

Consequently, I've never met, seen, spoken to, viewed a photo—or even a handwriting scrap—from my biological father.

When my mother married my father she did not know that he was a bigamist and embezzler, of course. But he was. And there she was in 1938, thousands of miles from her family, almost no friends, and saddled with a fatherless infant—decades before single motherhood became fashionable.

At the hospital where I was born and where she worked as a physical therapist, rumors spread about my illegitimacy. I understood more clearly the depth of my mother's humiliation and shame when, shortly before her death in 1990, she described putting her marriage license on the main hospital bulletin board to still those rumors. I am moved to tears even now when I think of the personal pain that action reveals.

As if her first marriage were not sufficiently wounding, two years later she married the alcoholic stepfather I believed was my birth father until Mother told me differently when I was ten. Mother divorced this stepfather three years later when his alcohol-related violence escalated to life-threatening levels.

Alcoholic Chaos

I'm still missing some chunks of my kaleidoscopically chaotic childhood in an alcoholic family. For instance, I have always remembered crawling out my bedroom window with my mom as my intoxicated stepfather bashed in the barricaded door with a hammer. But a few years before her death, she reminded me about us (my mom, baby brother, and me) sleeping in the family car because my stepfather locked us out. I had "forgotten" that impromptu family camp-out.

I blocked other memories too. For nearly three decades, I totally erased the horror and humiliation of sexual molestation at the hands of a stranger, family "friends," and—the worst—by a step-uncle.

How could those and many other frightening experiences occur when I had an extremely intelligent, well-educated, hard-working mom who loved me very much and loved God even more? Perhaps part of the answer is that my mother was also a very deeply shame-wounded woman. Her unseen wounds showed up most clearly in an inability to have a healthy, mutually respectful romantic relationship. This resulted in five marriages to four husbands.

Living the Shame

Alcoholic families are fertile seedbeds for shame. As the oldest child and "hero" I tried to fix the family and make my mother happy by being a good—no, make that a *perfect*— child. Naturally, I failed. Naturally too, with a child's limited logic, I blamed myself for not being good enough to do the impossible.

In addition, my shame-bound mother looked to her children to mend her tattered self-concept. As a result, she unintentionally conveyed that my achievements, which reflected well on her, were the most valuable things about me. This early emphasis on externals launched me into a lifetime of perfectionistic performing and pleasing to earn approval and love.

How did I cope as an imperfect and hurting person believing I was supposed to be (and often was *expected* to be) perfect and unwoundable to qualify for approval and love? I became a self-protective perfectionist and approval addict. (More details in subsequent chapters.) And I developed inner blindness. For you see, the unbiblical, life-crushing sense of shame that was binding me also was blinding me.

Binding shame breeds a kind of "existence guilt" when we believe only perfect people are eligible for life and happiness. When this is the case, we will be afraid to risk the honest self-examination necessary to have lives of authentic integrity and substantial wholeness. At least, that's how it was for me for most of my life.

All this was true even though I loved God and believed that he loved me. However, instead of lifting my heavy load of shame, what I believed about God actually *contributed* to it.

Problem 3: Believing God Doesn't Care About Our Unseen Inner Lives

Imagine with me for a moment what kind of deity would be most appealing to individuals bound up and blindfolded by shame: of course, a god who focuses totally on outward observance of prescribed religious rituals, because we're already familiar with a performance-based mindset and lifestyle. No wonder many of us sincere but shame-shackled Christians reshape the God of the Bible into *our* images by creating a deity disinterested in anything more than the externals. Yet I Samuel 16:7 says our Creator "looks at the heart" rather than "at the outward appearance," which—according to that same verse—is our human perspective.

When we filter Scripture through perceptual glasses bent and twisted by binding, blinding shame, we usually come up with a deity whose views are amazingly like our own! I now realize that I pulled off that theological sleight-of-hand for most of my faith life. However, God has this annoying habit of insisting I get to know him as he *really* is, and then allow him to be himself. (Maybe God is doing the same in your life.)

God has a very high opinion of truth. For example, Jesus—who is God "with skin on"—called himself truth in John 14:6. And, unlike humans who typically emphasize externals, God focuses primarily on our unseen, inner lives, or as Scripture usually terms it, our "hearts." Look at Proverbs 4:23 where we're told to "watch over" or "guard" our hearts because our external lives flow out of our internal selves—our "hearts." Jesus echoed this inner life focus in Mark 7:21 where he declared that all our visible behaviors spill out of our unseen inner lives—again, our "hearts."

So it's no surprise to discover that the God of truth who looks primarily at our hearts relentlessly calls us to lives of total truth—truth inside, where only he sees, and truth outside, where we relate to others. Yet many believers seem to be unfamiliar with God's desires for us to have "truth in [our] innermost beings." (See Psalm 51:6.)

In the June 1992, "Letters to the Editor" section of the Christian magazine *Moody Monthly*, the following appeared:

"It is ironic that your April issue [which featured excellent articles on the meaning of Christ's death and resurrection] also included a hodge-podge of psychology-based books. Do you believe it is wise to offer material that causes people to look inward instead of to 'Jesus the author and finisher of our faith?' "

Why must committed Christians be forced to do one or the other? (An example of all-or-nothing thinking at its most flagrant!) Why can't we do both? In fact, *God insists we do both!* So, I think God would say "Hooray" for articles and books that stimulate both.

As evidence of this consider that, in I Corinthians 11:28, God tells Christians to "examine" themselves before participating in the Lord's Supper. As I understand the examining process, it includes both looking inward at the condition of our "hearts," as truthfully as possible, and then looking to Jesus in faith to forgive the sin we discover, e.g., prolonging unforgiveness or murderous rage, nurturing adulterous thoughts, etc.

Did you notice that the examples of sin I suggested we might find during an inner examination are just a few of the hurtful ways we could respond to unseen emotional and relational wounds? We are not apt to let God give us wisdom into the "hidden parts" of our innermost beings to reveal these and other sinful, hurtful responses to unseen wounds when we believe he really wants us to ignore that "inside stuff." With this line of reasoning, we are apt to conclude that God sanctions and almost sanctifies an "anointed amnesia," more commonly known as denial of reality.

In Proverbs 28:13, God tells us that we will not "prosper" if we conceal our sins instead of admitting them and seeking forgiveness. Perhaps the same principle applies to unseen wounds when we continue to settle for hiding instead of healing.

Besides, when we hide from painful truths by clinging to our inner-sight blindfolds, we deprive ourselves of discovering that Jesus, the Great Physician, is as able to heal our unseen wounds as forgive our sins.

Pause to Ponder and Pray

PONDER: Read some or all of the following verses in more than one translation of the *Bible,* if possible. You may discover that God cares a lot more about our inward selves and our unseen wounds than most of us were ever taught.

✔ *Proverbs 4:23* (Compare with *Mark 7:21.* The "heart," i.e., thoughts, will, etc., is the source of everything others see and know of us.)

✔ *1 Samuel 16:7* (Note that God looks on our hearts. In effect, God goes to the source.)

✔ *Psalm 51:6* (God wants us to have truth at the source. He promises to give us wisdom in the inner parts of us that are hidden from our awareness.)

PRAY: Lord, you know that I have difficulty taking seriously what I can't see physically. So please anoint my inner eyes to see and please give me the courage to look. Please make me willing to commit to you my thoughts, feelings, and memories. Amen.

Just Ahead

We've seen that unseen wounds create problems that we usually try to ignore. Yet these wounds and their effects are powerful. We'll see why in Chapter Two.

CHAPTER
Two

The Power of
Unseen Wounds

"I'm just so tired of hurting!"

That's how Clarice, an exquisitely groomed, church-going, forty-something wife and mother answered my question about what brought her to counseling. (I have altered all names and personal details to conceal individuals' identities.) Clarice didn't limp, use crutches, or have a cast on her arm. On the contrary, she looked like she could have been poster girl for a "Good Life" promotion. But Clarice was hurting. And the inner pain was crippling her emotions and her dearest relationships.

Life brings wounds, both seen and unseen. And those wounds bring pain. Even when the wounds and the pain are unseen, they are not silent. In fact, in Proverbs 18:14, God implies that unseen wounds of the spirit are more difficult to bear than physical sickness. And it is precisely the reality and severity of that pain that gives unseen wounds their life-dominating power.

I think denial is so popular because reality can be so painful! Because that pain is powerful, it forces us to either face our wounds or employ increasingly potent pain-numbing devices. And both of those options create more pain when we're trapped in misbeliefs and myths.

If we are ever going to move from hurting to healing and helping, we need to look honestly at what we've been "my-thing." We started that process in Chapter One. Let's continue by examining additional misbeliefs that keep us stuck in cycles of hurts, wounds, pain, denial, and more hurts.

Misbelief 1: If I Look Honestly at My Wounds, I'll Blame and Dishonor My Parents

As we saw in the last chapter, looking honestly at our inner hurts is intended to provide an accurate context for making healthy changes in our lives. The old spiritual says, "Not my sister nor my brother but it's me, Oh Lord, standing in the need of prayer." Well, I am proposing a little variation on that theme that says, "Not my sister nor my brother nor my father nor my mother, but it's me, Oh Lord, standing up to take responsibility for my life!"

"Blaming" is actually an unhealthy variation on attributing responsibility. And truthful attribution of responsibility for our childhood environments points us straight to our parents. Anger may be an appropriate response to some of the choices our parents made. But if we never move beyond anger, it's like a race horse getting stuck in the starting gate. It's necessary to begin there, but we aren't supposed to stay there!

It really is possible to look inward and backward honestly, and then face, feel, and forgive what we find so that we can move forward into more truth-filled, balanced, Christ-honoring lives.

If you are feeling increasingly anxious or confused about now, it may be due to my use of the word *honestly*. After all, I'm supposed to be talking about honoring our parents. And for some of us, unfortunately, that topic seems to automatically preclude the concept of honesty.

Reconciling Honesty and Honoring

Lying is not a synonym for loyalty, or for love. And truth is not honor's enemy. The God who calls us to walk in inner and outer truth is the same God who tells us to honor our parents. So it must be possible to do both.

When I ask counselees and group members to define honor as they believe it applies to parents, they typically use the standard dictionary verbiage of "having great respect for" or "holding in high esteem." Obviously the more abusive parents have been, the more impossible seems the prospect of combining honesty with those definitions of honoring. That's exactly the impossible challenge that leads many people to believe they must choose between continued denial or great guilt over their failures to, for example, highly esteem their extremely impaired parents.

Several years ago I sought the expertise of my pastor, Dr. Ray DuPont, to help me understand the meaning of the word *honor* as it is used in the Commandment "honor your father and mother." (See Ex. 20:12.) In Hebrew, the word we translate *honor* originally meant "heavy" and "of great weight." Over time the word began to be applied to individuals, such as city officials, who were considered important and "weighty" because of their heavy influence.[1] This perspective on honor not only sheds new light, it opens cell doors for those imprisoned in misunderstanding. That's how it was for Clarice.

After Clarice began attending a church-sponsored group for adults raised in hurtful families, she became increasingly aware that years were missing from her childhood. Ages five through nine had always been "a total blank." But as she continued in the group, the thick veil over her missing years lifted here and there. Eventually the panicky confusion Clarice began to experience led her into counseling.

Jagged flashback fragments continued to form a mosaic of chronic hands-on and hands-off cruelty from her father, with the collusion of her passive, nonprotecting mother. As you've probably guessed, the worst of it came during Clarice's missing years. This is how she described her remembering and its emotional repercussions.

It was worse than any nightmare I had ever had, and believe me, I'd had some pretty wild ones. As more and more of the memories came, I thought I must be going crazy or making it all up. But my younger sister and a cousin remembered things that really validated my memories. As I finally let go of my denial, and asked God to let me know the truth, the grief poured over me. Before long, I realized that a big part of that grief included guilt that I wasn't honoring my parents like God wanted me to.

Clarice learned that she was honoring her parents more by honestly assessing their heavy influences in her life than by pretending they didn't carry such relational weight.

(c) 1988 by Mark Guerra

"EVERY TIME I COME HERE, I GET A STRANGE FEELING."

The cartoon depicts this powerful, pervasive inter-generational influence of parents on their children of all ages. Perhaps this is just a bit of an exaggeration. Perhaps.

Like Clarice, you may find that correctly understanding honor significantly smooths the path to increasing "wisdom in the hidden parts" of your inner being. But don't expect that journey to be free of rocky obstacles and potholes of misbelief. One of the most destructive misbeliefs actually shouts, "Get off that selfish inner-truth-seeking path right this minute!"

Misbelief 2: If I Deny My Wounds and Deaden My Pain, I Won't Be Self-focused

One of my favorite stories illustrates the subtle pitfalls of self-focused living.

A man was driving on a country road when a woman approached from the other direction. As she got near him, she rolled down her window, stuck out her head and began screaming, "Pig! Pig!" Now this guy was tired of all the women's-lib rhetoric describing men with that unflattering term, so he yelled back furiously, "Sow! Sow!" Pleased with his rapid retort, he rounded a curve and promptly plowed into a pig in the middle of the road.[2]

Self-focus makes us see all situations primarily as they relate to us, and every interaction becomes a commentary on our identities. The man in my story did that and ran into big trouble. So will we.

I've already acknowledged that the self-protective posture characterizing most of my adult life grew out of my shame-based self-focus. It was very difficult and painful for me to accept the truth about my self-centered approach to life, because one of a shame-based family's most powerful messages is that any attention to oneself is wrong.

Those of us who are Christians, as well as heirs of hurtful families, face an additional obstacle to owning our self-focus tendencies. We are usually busy focusing on not *appearing* self-focused so that our Christian friends won't think we're "unspiritual," "worldly," or "back-slidden." So between our legacies from shame-based families and our desires to avoid disapproval for "navel gazing," we are sitting ducks for the if-I-hide-my-wounds-and-numb-my-pain-I-won't-be-self-focused misbelief.

Getting Beyond Self-focus

A few years ago, my husband broke his leg at Riverfront Stadium while watching a Cincinnati Reds baseball game. What an evening! The couple we were with drove us to the emergency room of the closest hospital for X-rays, and a few days later Garth had surgery on his leg. You probably are not surprised to learn that Garth lived a pretty leg-focused existence for a while. Now just imagine that people whose approval Garth valued had begun telling him something like this:

> Some of us are concerned that you seem to be spending an *awful* lot of time and energy, even money, on your right leg these days. Don't you think all those resources would be better used serving others? I mean *all* of us have right legs, you know. You don't see *us* going around with crutches and big, flashy casts on *our* legs. And just look at all the extra work and stress your leg-focused life causes poor Sandy. If you'd call off your *pity party*, stand up on your own two feet, and be strong, you would be just fine. And devoting a little more time to prayer and Bible reading certainly wouldn't hurt either, you know. After all, this whole thing is really *your own fault*. If you hadn't been going after a foul ball with guys half your age, you wouldn't have gotten hurt. Besides, don't you realize that when people see you—a Christian—using a crutch and cast, you cause them to doubt Jesus' sufficiency to meet all your needs? Surely, you don't want to hurt the cause of Christ!

My husband does not normally lead a leg-focused life. However, wouldn't you agree that it was reasonable for him to become leg-focused rather quickly after his was broken? And don't you think it was wise of him to give his leg special attention, by having the prescribed surgery and physical therapy to speed the healing process so he could move beyond his temporarily leg-focused existence?

From a hurt-people-hurt-people perspective, I am suggesting that, to one degree or another, all of us have some type of broken, bruised, or injured limbs. This means that a certain degree of self-focus is inevitable. Said differently, considering our imperfection and our "woundability," the issue of self-focus is not a matter of *if,* but *how much* and *in what ways.*

Doesn't it make sense that if we will be purposefully and temporarily self-focused enough to honestly assess our injuries and take appropriate steps to recover healthy functioning, we will be much more likely to move beyond our self-*focus* into a realistic and healthy self-*awareness?* But if our fear of truth and/or disapproval binds us to ongoing denial of unseen wounds, we doom ourselves to continued focus on not appearing self-focused. And that is a miserable, exhausting way to live. Believe me, I know.

Misbelief 3: When I Won't Feel My Pain, It Won't Hurt You

I also know that when we knowingly or unknowingly deny the existence of our unseen wounds, rather than own and tend them, we are dangerous to others. And typically, we will hurt others most deeply in the areas of our own woundedness when we attempt to distance ourselves from our pain by deflecting it onto someone else.

This is how Annie describes being hurt by "deflected" pain.

"Joe (Annie's husband) and I have never made a secret of the fact that the Lord gave us Kathy Jo through the efforts of a Christian lawyer in a private adoption. Everybody in Joe's family and mine knows and understands and is really happy for us. I mean we'd tried for nine years to get pregnant. We didn't consider adoption until after all that time, tens of thousands of dollars in medical procedures and seeking God's will with our pastor and our Bible study praying for us. You can't imagine how shocked Joe and I were when his cousin called us 'black market baby buyers' in front of his entire family at the Christmas Open House."

(I'm interrupting Annie's story to let you peek into my head as I was listening to her. When I hear something like this, I automatically assume that the hurtfully inappropriate person is also a deeply hurting person who has been touched in a painful place. Now back to Annie.)

> "I was speechless and so was Joe. I mumbled something about everything being done legally and left the room as quickly as possible. Later, Joe's mom told me that, at seventeen, this unmarried cousin gave up a baby girl for adoption. I felt really sorry for her and was really glad she made the choice she did instead of having an abortion. But I was still crushed by what she said, and because she said it in front of the whole family."

Learning to see that this cousin was hurting, not just hurtful, helped Annie and Joe fully forgive and eventually reach out to her with genuine love.

It isn't unusual for hurt people to use anger to disguise and deflect their guilt and grief just as Joe's cousin did. Anger provides an illusion of personal power that may temporarily block feelings of confusion and helplessness common to painful personal crises. As unfairly wounding as this can be to others, there are even *more* hurtful ways of trying to numb "disowned" pain from unseen wounds.

WHEN VICTIMS BECOME VICTIMIZERS

Numerous studies have uncovered "a strong and direct relationship between chronicity of abuse experienced in childhood and adult abuse potential."[3] That sounds so dry and dispassionate, doesn't it? But if we bend our ears to the heartbeat of that statement, we hear the unmistakable roar of throbbing pain.

It seems to work like this: If I dominate and abuse you today, it helps me temporarily numb the intense pain I have because I was dominated and abused through many yesterdays. A sense of personal mastery through dominating someone even more powerless than oneself appears to be involved.

When we ponder such enormous ongoing wounding and pain, it can fuzz the lines between victim and victimizer to the point that we miss a crucial truth. *Understanding a behavior does not make it acceptable.*

Sometimes I need to be reminded of this indispensable chunk of reality to pull me out of the quicksand of easy empathy and plant me firmly on the Gibraltar of personal responsibility. The alternative is to duck our heads and pretend that no one can alter this intergenerational cycle. (Of course, we can always comfort today's victims by assuring them that their turns at victimizing come tomorrow.) Surely there has to be something better!

God has a name for the "something better." He calls it *wisdom*. In Proverbs 14:8 Scripture says that "wise" or "prudent" people give thought to their "ways," i.e., their manner of living. That mindset contrasts with the foolish who specialize in deception. I suspect that deception flows in two directions as we try to convince *ourselves and others* that we are strong, woundless and pain-free, instead of the needy, wounded and pain-touched people we, to some degree, are.

In Psalm 139:23–24 we find the answer to how self-deceptive folks like you and me could ever understand the true nature of our lives. Because the Psalmist sought that kind of truth about his manner of living, he asked God to search the source, his heart, to see if there were any "hurtful way" within him.[4]

I'll confess that I haven't always had the Psalmist's courage. How about you? Of course, when we lack understanding about our hurtful ways, we cannot make healthier, less hurtful life-choices. And so the cycle of hurts, wounds, pain and more hurts rolls on.

It's possible, of course, that everything you've read thus far could sound like a lot of self-serving psycho-babble. And I suppose it would be that, if our only goals were to justify our wounding ways with others and to achieve more comfortable lives for ourselves. But I have something more in mind.

Consider Wilson's Law of Relationships a declaration of universal human neediness and a call to the radical realism of total-person truth. I long for us to begin seeing through God's eyes by taking seriously unseen, inner injuries and wounds. Only then will we relate to ourselves and others with God's perspective on our "hurtful ways."

Pause to Ponder and Pray

PONDER: Have you ever heard comments like those of my husband's hypothetical "friends"? If so, who made those comments? You may want to consider spending less time around those folks if you are going to be spending more time seeking God's wisdom about your "hidden" inner being.

✔ Have you ever made comments like those? To whom?

✔ Take a moment to write down what you could say next time that would more accurately reflect God's perspective on inner injuries. (Review Prov. 18:14 for a reminder.)

✔ Do you think you may be wounding others because you haven't been willing to "own" your wounds? If so, whom are you wounding? How are you doing it?

PRAY: Lord, give me the wisdom to know if today is one of those times when I need to pay special attention to the wounds I can't see. Please teach me the difference between self-deception, self-indulgence, self-focus, and self-awareness. Amen.

Just Ahead

The thread of 1 Samuel 16:7's truth is woven throughout these first chapters—namely that God looks inside at people's hearts and we do not. Furthermore, nothing in our inner scenes is hidden from God. In contrast, not only can we not see into others' hearts, we cannot see the entire landscapes of our own inner territory with twenty/twenty accuracy. There are dark corners and deep caves where only God can give us wisdom.

A lot of that wisdom relates to our childhood experiences, and that means we need to look at our families. That's what we do next.

CHAPTER
Three

Hurt by the Unprepared
and Unavailable

"They did the best they could!"

Haven't you heard that said a hundred times in reference to parents? I think it is far more truthful to say that nearly all parents do the best they *know*, and no one is born knowing how to be a consistently adequate parent. When you stop to think about it, *our parents probably received more instruction for driving their cars than they did for parenting us*. No wonder even the most loving of them often floundered and even outright failed from time to time.

In this chapter, we will be exploring ways that well-meaning parents unintentionally inflict *hands-off hurts* by being either unprepared, unavailable or—more likely, a combination of both.

Hands-Off Hurts from Unprepared Parents

Some parents are more unprepared than others. For example, as my dear husband was driving me and our three-day-old firstborn home from the hospital, he glanced over and uttered these unforgettable words: "Do you know anything about taking care of a baby?" (I am not making this up!) While trying to muster an expression of indignation that he would even ask such a thing, I replied, "Of course."

I lied.

By contrast, the world's-most-adorable granddaughter is blessed with a mom and dad who spent a lot of time preparing for her arrival. (In case you haven't guessed, Garth and I became grandparents for the first time not long ago.) In addition to decorating and furnishing a darling nursery, our son and daughter-in-law read books, went to classes, and talked at length with their parenting-experienced friends about what to expect.

In parenting—or any other area of life, there's not a lot we can do to prepare for the unexpected, beyond *expecting* it. And although we know that parenting is packed with "unexpecteds," the truth is that there are even more "expecteds." One of these expectable aspects of parenting relates to what is commonly called *child development*, that is, the normal progression of physical, mental, and emotional changes that occur as children grow.

Unprepared parents often hurt their children unintentionally and needlessly by not understanding normal child development. The result can contribute to a sense of shame in the child.

Reinforcing Biological Shame

You may remember that I defined binding shame as a deep sense, i.e., both thoughts and feelings, that tells me I am different and worth *less* than other people. *Biological* shame is a *child's* sense of being different and worth less than adults, as a natural response to observable differences between children and grown-ups.[1]

As children, we *were* physically and intellectually "different and less than" our parents and other adults. Perhaps on some level of awareness, we may have believed that this condition was unique and eternal. If so, we may have assumed we were condemned to spend our entire lives *never* knowing how to solve the mysteries of muddy feet, Monopoly, or multiplication tables.

Because the basis of biological shame obviously is transitory, it has a 100 percent, fail-safe cure: *aging*. And at this point in our lives, we may be taller, stronger, and more highly skilled and educated than the very adults we once saw as giant geniuses.

If, in the normal course of maturing, children always outgrow the basis for biological shame, how could it become a source of unseen injury? The answer lies in the wounding that unprepared parents unknowingly cause with hurtful responses to a child's normal and expectable developmental limitations.

Here's an example of contrasting parental responses to the identical, absolutely expectable childhood behavior: a three-year-old's failure to keep pace with parent when shopping.

Hurtful and Shaming Response: "Why can't you keep up with me, you Slowpoke? Watch out, Clumsy, you bumped right into that lady's grocery cart. And stop wandering off all over the place. I haven't got all day, you know."

Helpful and Non-shaming Response: "You look like you're almost running to stay up with me. My legs are a lot longer than yours because I'm grown up, so I'd better slow down a little. I remember how hard it was for me to stay up with my mommy and daddy. Oops, we need to look out for the carts."

You get the idea. Children naturally walk more slowly, are less coordinated and more easily distracted than adults. These expectable developmental limitations disappear in time, and they need not be a source of shame for children. They won't be, if prepared parents understand and consistently adapt their expectations to child development patterns like the non-shaming parents in the example. In contrast, unprepared parents have unrealistic developmental expectations of children, and then they shame their children for not fulfilling them.

Unless developmental difficulties occur, children will find themselves one day on the adult side of life. Sadly, some of these adult children will carry inner scars from the hands-off hurts of unrealistic developmental expectations received from loving but unprepared parents.

And what's true about unrealistic *physical* development expectations almost always carries over to *intellectual* and *skill* developments as well. I know of an eight-year-old daughter harshly criticized—ridiculed actually—for not knowing how to follow a recipe, and a ten-year-old boy who received a similar parental response for not trimming hedges correctly. No adult had taken the time to teach these children how to accomplish their assigned tasks, but both were expected to perform perfectly.

Patient, persistent skill-building instruction takes time and energy. When parents carry their own set of small or large wounds, to one degree or another, the resulting pain distracts them and drains the emotional energy needed to instruct children repeatedly and appropriately according to their levels of development.

And distracted parents are unavailable parents.

Hands-Off Hurts from Unavailable Parents

I had two unavailable fathers. The first, my biological father, was unavailable because of desertion and divorce, and the second, my stepdad, through alcoholism and divorce. But you don't have to come from a single-parent family to know what it's like to be hurt by unavailable parents. In addition to divorce, desertion, and death, parents' personal problems and poor priorities can create "emotional orphans" in *zero*-parent homes.

Hurt by a Parent's Personal Problems

"Study: Scars from Abuse Can Last a Lifetime" screamed the headline of a recent newspaper article. Along with blatant acts of abuse, the story listed another form of parental treatment that research suggests contributes to a sharp drop in I.Q. and general functioning between ages one and two in the children studied.

"These were kids who, because of *the emotional unrespon-siveness of their parents*, lost interest in exploring their environment, [the primary researcher] said."[2] Does that sound melodramatic and overstated? If so, you may be surprised to learn that what this recent research found is actually "old news." (Now there's an oxymoron as self-contradictory as jumbo shrimp!) Even Job knew about unavailable parents:

> If his sons are honored, he does not know it;
> If they are brought low, he does not see it.
> He feels but the pain of his own body and mourns only for himself. (Job 14:21-22 NIV)

What an extraordinary foreshadowing of the truth about the wounds children sustain from emotionally unavailable parents! We see a father so distracted by his personal pain that he notices neither his sons' achievements nor their afflictions. This dad really is *emotionally unresponsive*.

Consistent with my entire hurt-people-hurt-people premise, I contend that parents can be just as self-absorbed and emotionally unavailable from painful personal problems that are *not physical in origin*. I am only too familiar with this reality from my early parenting days, when deep depression left me emotionally unavailable to Becky and Dave for about six months.

You may not be able to relate to "weak and needy" depressed or despondent parents at all. In fact, your folks may have been extremely successful, high energy, go-get-em kinds of people. If so, don't be surprised to discover that you also can have inner hands-off hurts.

Hurt by Parents' Poor Priorities

Some of us grew up in families where one or both parents were nearly always "too busy," "too tired," or "too important" to be available.

This pattern is very common in ministry homes: of pastors, missionaries, denominational leaders, seminary professors, parachurch personnel and other ministry types—including therapists, speakers and authors. (Did I just hear someone say "Ouch?") Jeff was intimately acquainted with this source of unseen wounds.

"Did you ever think of the telephone as a lethal weapon?" Jeff's intense brown eyes searched my face for a reply. But before I could voice one he continued, "I grew up dreading the sound of the phone in our home, because every time it rang it meant 'death' to any hope of spending time with my folks—especially my dad. He wasn't a bad guy at all. In fact everyone in our town thought he was great. He was a successful real estate broker, an elder at church, and he headed the local branch of a well-known Christian organization. It's just that he never had time to do stuff with me, you know, stuff like go to my soccer games or really talk to me. I mean *really* talk."

Jeff's childhood experience certainly is not new or unique. In fact, the kind of families Jeff described are epidemic in our hurried, harried, pressure-cooker society. And in our society-pressured churches. When I hear about parents who wound out of their success instead of their suffering, so to speak, I think of an amazing true story I heard.

One of my friends had an unexpected travel adventure a few years ago when she and her husband moved to a Midwestern community. The first time she road the city bus, she all but suffered whiplash as it raced around corners and zoomed down streets even faster than most of the cars. When she got to the station at the end of her ride, she asked the driver why he went so fast.

He explained that when city bus service began, administrators had the drivers run practice trips to determine route times, and the bus schedule was printed accordingly. There was only one little problem. On the practice trips, the drivers forgot to actually *stop* at the designated bus stops and allow time for loading and unloading passengers! *In effect, the drivers forgot to factor in the very purpose for which the bus line existed!*

Families exist for the purpose of meeting genuine needs. One of the most important of these needs is parental nurturing of children. That God-designed enterprise takes time and even some "unscheduled stops" along the way. However, many "successful" people treat their children as inconvenient impediments to be dispatched with as little time and personal attention as possible so that the parents can get on with their schedules full of "important things."

My guess is that the vast majority of these emotionally unavailable, unrealistically overscheduled parents would raise a chorus of, "But I never meant to hurt my kids." So why did they? The answer is wrapped up in the fact that, to their children, these—and *all*—parents are mirrors with messages.

Messages from Marred Mirrors

As children, the image of ourselves we saw mirrored in our parents' faces and in their behavior toward us became the nucleus around which our identities developed. This is why "*self*-images" fundamentally are *mirror*-images. In effect, we lived in Snow White's zip code.

"Mirror, Mirror, on the wall, who's the fairest of them all?" The evil queen in *Snow White* knew she would always hear the truth when the magical talking mirror answered her question about the identity of the kingdom's "fairest." And similarly, as children we possessed "talking mirrors"—we called them Mommy and Daddy. As children, we assumed that our "talking mirrors" always told the truth too. That's why we received without reservation what we saw mirrored in our parents' faces as the exact reflection of our true identities and worth. I know I believed that. Didn't you?

When we were very young we lacked the reasoning sophistication necessary to understand that, in reality, what we saw in our parents' faces and heard in their voices reflected who *they* were, not who *we* were. And we had no way of knowing that even the most loving parents can become extremely marred mirrors when they are unprepared with basic child development information and/or are unavailable because of personal pain or poor priorities. And, as if those parenting struggles weren't enough, we need to remember that, to some extent, our folks also bore scars and pain from unseen wounds received from *their* scarred and hurting parents. All these difficulties and personal issues produce static, garbling our parents' well-intentioned messages.

Listening to the Messages We Received

In hurtful families normal childhood behavior often elicits wounding responses from parents operating out of unrealistic developmental expectations and perfectionistic demands. And these wounding responses send loud, clear identity messages to their children. In effect, a child's imperfect and awkward or inappropriate behavior becomes a definitive statement about that child's identity and worth.

The following chart displays several examples of typical childhood behavior, and includes helpful and hurtful parental responses along with the identity messages children likely "hear" from each response. As you read it, ask yourself which statements sound more familiar as you recall your childhood.

Contrasting Parental Responses and "Messages" They Send

HELPFUL RESPONSE	MESSAGE	HURTFUL RESPONSE	MESSAGE
SITUATION: Three-year-old is wriggling in restaurant "booster chair"			
"Look at the pretty color crayons they gave you. Here, you can color on your placemat."	My folks like me and they help me find interesting things to do.	"Stop that wriggling. Sit up straight. How many times do we have to tell you to behave yourself, you little brat."	I can't be the way I should be. I don't make my folks happy. I am a brat.
SITUATION: Kindergartener spills a glass of milk at breakfast			
"Oh dear, there goes the milk. Paper towels will soak that up in a jiffy. I think maybe I filled your glass too full."	Paper towels are good for cleaning up spilled milk.	"Oh great, as if I didn't have enough to do. You are always so clumsy and careless. What a mess!"	I am always a clumsy and careless person. I make messes and am a lot of bother to people.

HELPFUL RESPONSE	MESSAGE	HURTFUL RESPONSE	MESSAGE
SITUATION: Fourth-grader leaves model airplane materials on dining table			
"I need you to clean up your model building things so I can set the table. Let's see if we can find a special place for your projects."	I am expected to clean up after myself. My interests are important.	"You are always such a selfish slob. Just look at all this junk you left in here."	I am a selfish slob. My interests and things are junk.
SITUATION: Ten-year-old reminds dad about Pee Wee League game			
"Hey, Sport, I wouldn't miss it. You really look like you're having a great time with the team this year. Am I right?"	My dad thinks I am important. He wants me to enjoy myself when I play baseball.	"Yeah, well I know I promised to come but I'm just too busy with this project. All you do is strike out anyway."	I am bad to want Dad to come to my games. I am not as important as his work. I am not good enough to earn his attention.

The first two examples of "hurtful responses" relate to parents who are unprepared to react appropriately to their children because they don't recognize developmentally appropriate behavior. In each of the first two examples, the parents are requiring and expecting their children to behave as if they were actually older than they are. These children are receiving a command that is impossible to obey, namely, be someone different than you are. That's a lot like telling a brown-eyed child, "Be blue-eyed."

Impossible-to-satisfy expectations deliver hurtful, wounding messages to the children who receive them. If a child consumes a steady diet of such impossible expectations and wounding self-concept messages, that child comes to believe that some unique, soul-deep, fundamental flaw dooms him or her to a lifetime of never measuring up. Can you recognize any of this dynamic and damage in yourself?

The second two examples of "hurtful responses" reflect parents who have poor priorities. (Obviously there is considerable overlap of unprepared and unavailable parent issues in all four examples of hurtful responses.) Parents need to be available enough to their children to help them find room and time for their activities and interests. And, of course, when dads or moms are too preoccupied with projects at home or at the office, they are unavailable to their children.

Unavailable Parents Mean Unmet Needs

All children have needs which they express to their adult caregivers, such as, the need for emotional security and nurturing that comes from a safe, gentle embrace. Children have many other needs too, for example, the need for parental attention and companionship. When parents are unavailable because of personal problems or poor priorities, they may want to—even promise to—meet their children's needs, sincerely intending to do just that. But these unavailable parents are unlikely to follow through on pledges of time devoted to children's activities.

Feeling the pain of unmet needs and faced with a string of broken promises, a child begins to believe that there is something wrong with his or her needs, instead of understanding that there is something wrong with the parent's commitment to promise-keeping. What's more, as young children we were unable to separate our needs and feelings from our very selves, i.e., from our personhood.

As a result, if we had unavailable parents who consistently treated our needs, interests, and feelings as unimportant and unworthy of their attention and time, we likely learned to see ourselves as unimportant and unworthy of our parents' care. Confronted with such a deeply wounding situation, many of us determined to somehow become good enough to be noticed and loved.

Bill developed an interest in body building, "to make my dad proud of me," he said. Apparently Bill's father was quite the successful athlete, and he expected no less of his sons. But Bill was a big disappointment to Dad. He was not particularly well-coordinated and just did not excel at any sport like his older brothers did. So Bill began lifting weights and discovered that didn't require much coordination—just a lot of determination and hard work. And steroids produced amazing results.

At the time I saw Bill's story on television, he had been off the steroids about a year because of severe liver and kidney damage. When the interviewer asked why he kept using steroids after knowing about their damaging side effects, Bill said he had to. He wanted to win at higher and higher levels of competition.

"Winning was that important to you? So important you'd risk your health?"   The reporter's incredulous question brought this reply. "Well, I guess it does sound crazy. But I just kept hoping that if I won a more important competition, it would make my dad proud of me." At the very end of the segment, the reporter asked Bill if his father was proud of his body-building achievements. Bill replied that *his dad had never once come to see him compete, not even when he won a "Mr. Universe of Body-Building" type title.*

Bill had focused his entire existence on winning the attention and approval of his father, on getting "The Parental Seal of Approval." As many of you know, that seal is much more elusive than the *Good Housekeeping* Seal of Approval! Bill even risked his health and permanently damaged his body in a desperate attempt to earn his dad's you-are-important-enough-to-notice-and-love message.

I wish I could talk to Bill. I'd tell him that it's fine to compete for body-building titles if that interests you. But I don't think that Bill—or any other child, was ever meant to compete for a parent's love. When children grow-up believing they should, they bear unseen wounds.

Pause to Ponder and Pray

PONDER: Complete the following to help you "hear" your parental talking mirrors. Remember, most parents love their children and do the best they *know*.

✔ As a child, I was good when _____
✔ As a child, I was bad when _____

PRAY: Lord, please help me to remember that my folks are/were imperfect, hurting people just like me. Remind me that lying is not loving, and make me willing to seek truth more than approval. Amen.

Just Ahead

As we've seen, children naturally believe that those "giant geniuses" we call Mommy and Daddy *know* the truth about everything and that they always *tell* the truth about everything. And as we've also seen, this situation can create some distortions in what we learn about ourselves, since even great parents aren't perfect parents.

However, there is a major difference in the degree to which truth is twisted when the hurtful messages are not from mildly "marred mirrors," but from outright liars and thieves. We examine that painful situation next.

CHAPTER
Four

Hurt by
Liars and Thieves

Bright yellow ribbons still fluttered from the porch of a Detroit home when the returning Persian Gulf War veteran they had welcomed died in front of his own house. He escaped Middle-Eastern enemies and scud missiles, only to be shot to death by his wife and her brother.

We don't expect soldiers to survive combat and return home to be cut down by their next of kin. Yet some families maneuver in battlefields more deadly than those officially designated war zones, as was the case for the murdered Persian Gulf veteran. But most of the time, since there are no *visible* corpses, we can't always spot these "fatal families" that routinely slaughter children's self-concepts, hopes, and dreams.

As we've seen in previous chapters, to one degree or another, all parents are hurt people. And, to one degree or another, all parents are hurting other people. Hurting parents are most hurtful to the helpless, tiny, trusting people born into their families—their own children. Most parents work hard to provide loving, appropriate care for their children. Other parents miss that mark when they are unprepared or unavailable. But parents who neglect and abuse their children actually are liars and thieves!

Parents function as liars and thieves for many reasons that all have a common denominator: unresolved, personal, life-dominating problems. The problems might be caused by chemical dependency or emotional instability, such as chronic, untreated depression or "rageaholism," or by many other sources. The results, however, are always the same for the children: With varying degrees of intensity, the children are wounded because their profoundly impaired parents do not provide consistently adequate care.

This chapter describes some of the ways in which neglect and abuse can deeply wound and even traumatize children who grow up in war-zone households headed by adults who live and parent like lying bandits.

Parents Wound Their Children by Stealing

Significantly impaired parents rob their offspring in many ways. Parental thieves steal overall security and stability, physical and sexual safety, and the capacity to trust in severely unhealthy, hurtful families.

Stealing Childhood Security and Stability

Have you ever stopped to consider that while it is illegal to rape or murder a child, it is not against the law to steal a childhood? Now, I think that's a crime!

A great philosopher once said that the most important question we ever ask and answer is: "Is the universe a safe place?" Parents create the earliest universes their young children inhabit. In healthy families, these worlds are secure and stable places where the bigger, more knowledgeable citizens (parents) truthfully answer the spoken and unspoken questions and meet the needs of the smaller, less sophisticated inhabitants (children).

Unless some unforeseeable financial crisis intervenes, children in well-functioning families can expect to live under a roof where they receive food when they are hungry, larger clothes when they outgrow what they have, and medical attention as needed. Neither the roof, the food, the clothing, nor the health care need be luxurious; consistently adequate will do.

God takes this parental responsibility very seriously. That's not surprising when we consider that the family is the God-designed human instrument for meeting basic physical needs. For example, in 1 Timothy 5:8, God leads the apostle Paul to tell a young church leader, "If anyone does not provide for his own, and especially for those of his household, he has denied the faith and is worse than an unbeliever." That's pretty strong language.

Unfortunately some impaired parents reorder family priorities with weird and wounding results. A man I'll call Ted was raised on a farm where his father, a prominent authority on agriculture and animal husbandry, fed his show animals far better than his sons and daughters. Ted vividly recalls fighting over a piece of fruit with his sisters and brother while the feeding troughs in the barn overflowed.

Just as the parents' provision of basic material needs establishes an atmosphere of fundamental security in a family, the parents' performance of leadership roles provides a sense of family stability. Significantly impaired parents routinely abdicate their leadership roles in their hurting, hurtful families.

"Childified" Adults Create "Adultified" Children

It is not uncommon these days to see adult offspring caring for, and making decisions about, their elderly parents. While better planning on the parents' part might reduce much of this burden on their adult children, some of this parent-child role-reversal is unavoidable. However, irresponsible, immature parents using their young and adolescent children to fill gaps in family leadership is an entirely different situation.

"I was so terrified!" That's how Jenny described her feelings when at age six she had to snatch her baby brother from his crib, call the fire department, and then try to drag and shove her over-tranquilized mother (who had fallen asleep with a cigarette in her hand) out of the house. In less dramatic cases, children of seven or eight, or even younger, frequently cook for themselves and younger siblings, wash their own clothes, and generally try to parent, while their parents are absorbed with jobs, affairs, depression, legal or illegal substances, church activities, or some combination of these preoccupations.

These upside-down families are mildly to overwhelmingly frightening, not only to the parent-impersonating children in charge, but also to their brothers and sisters. Young children figure out pretty early that "kids are us" and that kids (even older kids) are not really intended to be, or adequate to be, parents.

I have a theory about what happens when young children discover that their security is in jeopardy because the family's stability rests in the shaky hands of irresponsible parents or has been passed off to the tiny hands of other children. In these circumstances, young children—even infants—begin early to focus on staying alive by trying to keep themselves safe.

I don't think it's much of a stretch for us to also assume that in more secure, stable families, children are going to have the chance to develop in healthier ways. After all, keeping oneself safe drains a lot of energy that could go into developing creativity and healthy confidence. Since safety is our most basic need, it ought to be a given in families. Sadly, it isn't.

Stealing Childhood Safety

There's a phrase in Hebrews 11:32 that perfectly expresses my thoughts as I approach the topic of child-unfriendly, unsafe families: "And what more shall I say? I do not have time to tell about . . ." (NIV). Truly, I grow weary of collecting newspaper and magazine articles and weeping over stories from counselees and seminar attenders that tell of horrendous, often unspeakable, examples of physical and sexual abuse suffered at the hands of parents, grandparents, and other family caregivers. My "Child Abuse" file is bulging, my heart is breaking, and there is no end in sight.

My husband uses the term *no-brainer* for situations that are so obvious they don't require any mental energy to explain or understand. Wouldn't you agree that expecting children's arms, legs, and genitals to be safe in their own homes is a *no-brainer?* Oh, how I wish it were!

Stealing Physical Safety

Recently I heard a heartbreaking story about a six-year-old boy who lives in an extremely violent neighborhood where gunshots routinely punctuate the rhythm of daily life. One evening as the lad's mother was putting him to bed, she noticed an empty deodorant bottle on his bedside table. When she asked him to explain, he replied, "It [the label] says it is guaranteed to keep me 100 percent safe."

As traumatic as it is for children to grow up where violence reigns outside the walls of home, it is far more devastating and dangerous when safety bandits rule inside the home. Some blatant examples of physical child abuse are:[1]

- Slapping, shaking, scratching, sticking with pins

- Squeezing tight enough to cause pain

- Hitting or beating with boards, sticks, belts, kitchen utensils, yardsticks, electrical cords, hoses, shovels, etc.

- Throwing, pushing, shoving, or slamming against walls, floors, or objects

- Burning, scalding, freezing, holding under water

- Confining in closets, basements, attics, boxes, locked rooms

- Withholding food or water

Unfortunately, this list is representative—not exhaustive. Some safety thieves are quite obvious, but other parents steal safety more subtly.

Twelve-year-old Tom's drawing on the next page illustrates "vicarious abuse." This phrase acknowledges that

when you witness anyone else being abused, you are a victim
of that abuse also. Even when a pet, piece of furniture, or
part of your house received a violent adult's blows, as a
child—somewhere in the corner of your mind—you feared
that next time *you* would be the punching bag.

Another subtle type of hands-off physical child abuse is
verbal violence.

Verbally violent families may never come to actual physical blows, but kids grow up hearing statements like, "If you
say another word, I'll cram my fist down your throat." (Does
any of this sound familiar to you?)

Physical safety is not the only casualty in significantly
unhealthy families. Some parents also steal sexual safety
and slay sexual innocence in the process.

Stealing Sexual Innocence and Safety

Current estimates suggest that one in four girls and one
in seven boys will be victims of sexual abuse before the age
of eighteen. Most of us have heard those facts so often we
have become desensitized to the hurt and horror they express.

In well over 90 percent of the cases reported, the abuser is
someone acquainted with the child. This means that while
children need to be warned about "stranger danger," family

members and trusted authority figures actually pose the greatest threats to children's sexual safety.

I know the truth of that statement only too well. I was molested by the stereotypical "dirty old man" stranger when I was seven. But the most painful sexual abuse episode came at the hands of my stepuncle the summer of my eleventh birthday. I totally blocked all memory of that terrifying experience for over three decades.

Like many adults who are victims of incest, I did not identify myself as an incest survivor because I narrowly defined incest as sexual intercourse only. Voices in Action, a self-help organization for incest survivors, defines incest as "a betrayal of trust involving overt or covert sexual actions—direct or indirect, verbal or physical (which may include, but is not limited to, intercourse)—between a child and a trusted adult and/or authority figure." That trusted person might be a parent, grandparent, stepparent, babysitter, older sibling, mom's boyfriend, teacher, pastor, family doctor, coach, or Scout Leader.

To better understand incest, we need to know that it is far more about the insecure, immature abuser's need to dominate and control than it is about sex *per se*. The incest offender is trying to meet emotional intimacy needs with someone he (most perpetrators are male) can control and dominate. By being sexual with someone less powerful—a child—the abuser eliminates the possibility of being rejected by a more suitable adult partner or spouse. This need to create the illusion of being desired explains why many incest perpetrators force their victims to say, "I love you," "I like this," or something similar, during or immediately after the abuse.

Like physical abuse, sexual abuse takes many forms. The following is a list of some of them:

- Sexual innuendos, jokes, comments, looking, leering
- Sexual stimulating, fondling, and touching
- Exposing self to or masturbating in front of the child
- Mutual masturbation

- Oral, anal, or vaginal intercourse (*rape* is the more accurate term)

- Penetration with finger or objects

- Stripping and sexual punishments (such as enemas, attaching wires to genitals)

- Forcing children to have sex with each other or with animals

- Watching others have sex or be abused sexually

- Sexual "games" or torture (for example, burning)

- Pornography—taking pornographic pictures of a child or forcing the child to watch pornography

Appendix A contains a Survivor's Traits list. You may be surprised to find that many of the distressing, confusing issues you struggle to cope with are the direct result of abuse when you were a child, rather than proof that you are weird or some kind of "bad seed."

Remember that some forms of incest are subtle, hands-off abuses and, therefore, even more confusing than overt incest. For example, Carla remembers that in her strict, very religious family, she and her two sisters were called whores for wearing slacks or shorts. This kind of sexualizing of nonsexual behavior is common in many homes where no overt sexual abuse ever takes place. In these homes mixed messages about sexuality abound. They may not all be as blatant as "Sex is filthy and disgusting; save it for the one you love and marry!" But they are misleading, confusing, unbiblical, and extremely unhealthy messages about human sexuality.

Incest survivors often feel like damaged goods. And if they do not remember any childhood abuse, they have no way of making sense of their self-hatred and shame. (Remember, shame is the sense that "I am different from, and worth *less* than, others.") You probably won't be surprised to learn that sexual and physical abuse survivors also have problems trusting appropriately. That makes perfect sense, because those crimes against children are fundamentally betrayals of trust.

Stealing Children's Trust

Parents and other adult authority figures who neglect and abuse children are *trust bandits*. They steal children's capacity for appropriate trust. The result has a profound effect on the children's later relationships with God, as well as with other people. Sometimes the scars from deep trust-betrayal wounds show themselves in the most unlikely ways in the most unlikely people. Many of us assume that deeply wounded adults bleed, so to speak, obvious personal dysfunction all over their lives. But actually most of them (dare I say *us?*) look amazingly all put together. Consider the remarkable story of Gunther Gebel-Williams, the renowned animal trainer with the Ringling Brothers and Barnum and Bailey Circus.

Gebel-Williams grew up hating his alcoholic father. So he says he felt no regret when his father did not return from World War II. In the years just after the war, however, Gebel-Williams and his mother nearly starved in battle-scarred Germany until, when he was thirteen, his mother sold him to a small European circus.

He became committed to animal training, even though he was mauled severely many times by lions and tigers. He says that people "may disappoint you, but animals never do. You know from the beginning if they like you or they don't." Consequently this world-famous, highly-respected, he-man circus star finds it easier to trust his big cats than to trust people.

Why? Even though it's been half a century since his mother abandoned him, "It still hurts. . . ."[2]

What dramatic evidence for the die-hard staying-power of unseen wounds!

When Parents Lie

Bandit-parents send loud and clear messages. And these messages overflow with lies.

Some lies are more destructive than others. Two relatively benign untruths, *easy to assemble* and *one size fits all*, for example, usually perpetrate only minor inconvenience or embarrassment. However, more malignant lies, such as "I can do anything I want because I'm your parent" and "You are disrespecting your elders when you object to Grandpa's wet kisses," wound deeply.

Lies About Children's Normal Needs and Personal Worth

I have counseled with many adults who live downwind from the toxic belief-system fallout of perpetrator-defined realities. One of the most common of these abuser-twisted "truths" takes a child's normal nurturing need for cuddles and physical touch and relabels it sexual come-ons. Incest perpetrators choose this devastatingly destructive deception in a pathetic, but usually successful, attempt to shift responsibility for sexual child abuse from themselves to the child.

Think of how easily a child could be fooled into believing that her natural, human need to be held and cuddled was her way of "asking for it." "It," of course, would be some form of incest that child would be told, and would probably believe, she caused. And abusers' lies redefine reality about children's personal worth as well as their natural needs.

"As long as I can remember, my dad has called me a slut," whispered Lynn, a petite, mid-thirtyish homemaker who is a committed Christian. She sought counseling originally to work on depression and low self-esteem issues that rapidly became despair and intense self-hatred issues. After some months, this bright, caring woman began to experience frightening memory fragments flashing through her mind. These episodes were followed by intense feelings of terror and a sense that "something awful" was about to happen.

The puzzle pieces of Lynn's previously unremembered childhood eventually fell together, revealing at least seven years of violent incest. And this is where her dad's "slut" references connect. From age three, when her father began to rape and sodomize her, she heard herself called a slut.

Lynn didn't know what a slut was. She only knew that because she was one, it was all right for Daddy to do those painful things "in front and in back—and in back hurt *so* bad."

"It was such an awful, hopeless feeling," Lynn told me while tears streamed mascara tracks down her cheeks. "You see, I didn't know what I did that made me a slut. And, even worse, I didn't know how *not* to be a slut so he would stop doing those hurtful things."

Like all of us, Lynn needed to have a million questions answered when she came into this world. She needed to know, for example, "Who am I?" and "Is the world a safe place?" But tragically Lynn's lying caregivers taught her that she was a slut and that so-called fact disqualified her from living in a safe world.

Parents who abuse or fail to protect their offspring from known abuse (as Lynn's mother did) clearly perpetrate a hideous hoax that misrepresents nearly every aspect of personal and family life.

Lies About What's Normal

Children in severely abusive families learn a lot of crazy-making lies about what constitutes normal conduct for individuals and families. These are a few of the most common "what's normal" lies.

The abuse is normal; therefore, your distressing emotional response is wrong and you are bad for having those feelings.

Parents use this lie to minimize and normalize their abusive, emotionally abandoning behavior. It is not unusual for me to hear counselees describe being accused of being "too sensitive" when they mustered the courage to object to such treatment. I've counseled with incest survivors who, when they began to recall their childhood sexual abuses, were told by family members, "That was just his way of showing affection." "He" might have been Uncle Joe, Grandpa, or Dad. And "his way" may have included masturbating to orgasm in front of the child, fondling the child's genitals, or even oral, anal, or vaginal rape.

Such families remind me of an incident that occurred in a small Midwestern community after several high-school girls murdered a classmate. They had sodomized her with a crowbar, slashed her legs with razor blades, bludgeoned her, and then incinerated her while she was still alive. In the article describing this unbelievably grisly murder, one featured spokesperson represented worried business owners concerned that the town's tourist traffic would decline. What struck me most was the term used by the image-preserving, tragedy-minimizing townspeople to describe the incident. They referred to it as *"The Unpleasantry"*!

Words are powerful tools to convey or conceal truth. Hurtful families use words to both minimize and discount genuine abuse and to redefine appropriate victim response as "making a federal case of it" or "causing trouble."

The abuse is normal and justified because there is some basic flaw or evil in you that causes the abuse.

As adults, we immediately label this lie as utter garbage. But young children believe their parents know everything about everything and that they always tell the truth. What a heavy, hurtful heritage this lie becomes!

The abuse is normal and necessary for the family. In fact, the world is a better place when you are being abused.

Many incest survivors recall their abusers saying that if anyone learned about the incest the family would break up and it would all be the child's fault. The message? It is good for the family when the child gets hurt.

It is normal to focus totally on maintaining the public image that we are a perfectly happy, problem-free family, while simultaneously ignoring all evidence to the contrary.

The first three of these "what's normal" lies are core curricula in hurting and hurtful families. But this fourth one is a supremely important lie that must be carefully taught and thoroughly learned in what I call "moon families."

I've heard that on planet Earth we see only one side of the moon, while its dark side is visible only via space exploration. There are moon-like families who carefully conceal their dark sides from public view. These appearance-addicted moon families, are extremely confusing to children, who are at a loss to make sense of the world when they hear others say how wonderful, even godly, their abusive parents are. By the way, Jesus had some pretty scathing words for the appearance-addicted religious leaders of his day. You'll find his words recorded in Matthew 23:25–28. I see no reason why

his attitude would be any different concerning family leaders
of our day.

Homes where parents act one way in public and a different
way in private remind me of an incident that occurred near
my home. A fellow hired a hit man to kill his estranged wife.
This homicidal husband was a professional clown![3] (I am not
making this up!) It boggles my mind to contemplate a *killer
clown*. Who would ever suspect a clown of being a killer?
Only those who get close enough to see beneath his grease-
paint and into his heart could possibly guess.

In much the same way, I believe that if we could look into
the hearts of abusive parents, we would discover a life-shaping lie about parental authority.

Lies About Parental Authority

Do you believe parents have the right to raise their children without any outside interference? Think carefully before you answer.

I know we live in a day when governmental agencies
encroach little by little into family life, threatening to erode
parents' rights to raise their children according to personal
beliefs. However, even a cursory reading of today's newspaper is enough to convince us that parental rights must be
reasonably tempered with child concerns.

To be sure, there have been abuses of child protection laws
and agencies. Nevertheless, most of us would agree that
when parents neglect or abuse children, someone needs to
step in and help those children. Some parents believe the
right to control their children is inalienable and inviolate,
and some of the families they lead become, in effect, *Dark
Kingdoms*.

Dark Kingdom Families

In Dark Kingdom households, deception and destruction
rule, and offspring exist for the sole purpose of meeting the
parents' needs. A kind of "paper towel mentality" exists
regarding children: Use them and throw them away.

I once worked with a counselee who had survived a devastatingly dark kingdom childhood filled with incest, physical

torture, and satanic ritual abuse. It was not unusual for her to leap from a comfortable chair in the counseling office and huddle in a corner behind the wastebasket. At those times she was reliving the countless dehumanizing childhood experiences when she was told that she was garbage and, therefore, she deserved to eat garbage. As unbelievable as it may sound, many days as a child she was given nothing to eat but garbage and human waste.

How do children survive the soul-deep wounds of such intense moral and spiritual darkness? This heroic counselee coped, in part, by dividing the horrors of her home life into many memory fragments separated by amnesiac barriers. Her capacity to dissociate, that is, to disconnect her mind from her body and her unbearable circumstances, saved her sanity and her life.

Sometimes I encounter Dark Kingdom refugees at conferences. Occasionally, they follow up our brief conversations with letters. A few months ago I received a ten-page letter from such a survivor (I'll call her Renata) after she heard me speak at an inner-city Chicago church. In the letter Renata described a childhood of repeated abuses, including her father's desertion and incest at the hands of her uncle. Here are two paragraphs from my response:

> Your father and your uncle were *liars and thieves!* With their words and with their actions they told you that you are worthless and deserve to exist only for their convenience (when fathering responsibilities got inconvenient, your dad walked out) or pleasure (your uncle made your precious little girl body into his sexual gadget). That is a hideous lie! You are a beautiful, unique, special creation of God. There will never be another human being exactly like you. And they both stole the safety, security, and stability that responsible, healthy adults rightfully attempt to provide for the children in their care.
>
> *Please remember that their treatment of you is not a statement about something missing and wrong in you, Renata. It is a statement about something missing and wrong in them.*

This beautiful Christian sister and countless others I've counseled or met are all survivors in the finest, truest sense of that word.

Yellow Ribbons for Survivors of Liars and Thieves

On the desk in front of me is a bright yellow brochure published by VOICES in Action, Inc., an organization for child abuse survivors. The last page of the brochure includes the following thoughts, under the heading, "Yellow Ribbons for Survivors."

> Adults who survived physical and/or sexual abuse or neglect as children are as deserving of yellow ribbons as are the men and women of our armed forces and consular corps who were held hostage in Iran. Indeed, many of those adults were taught how to survive confinement, separation from people who cared about them, abuse and/or neglect. The child who is victimized by a trusted authority figure is held captive not by foreigners but by her or his own family. And the only resources that child has to rely on are internal. If you are a victim of child sexual [or physical] abuse, we applaud your survival and encourage you to buy a yellow ribbon for yourself. You—above all—deserve it.

I agree, my friend. *You do deserve it!*

Pause to Ponder and Pray

PONDER: Even though it may be very difficult and painful, I invite you to turn to Appendix A if you have not done so already. Remember that many of the traits listed are not unique to incest survivors. Some, such as hypervigilance, are common to survivors of both physical *and* sexual battering. Other traits, such as chronic depression, may show up in adults who were never severely neglected or abused.

Here are some suggestions to make this exercise most helpful:

✔ Before you read (or reread) the list of survivor traits, ask God to prepare your mind to receive the truth he desires to reveal at this time. Be honest about your fear, anger, sadness, or whatever emotion you are feeling right now. (God won't be shocked or surprised!)

✔ As you read, mark the traits that "feel like" you. (You may want to record these in a journal rather than in this book.) Remember, clusters of traits are more indicative of abuse than are isolated traits.

If, as you started reading the list, you felt too dizzy, light-headed, nauseated, or generally confused to finish, discuss this with your counselor, if you have one. If you don't have one, and if you continue to be "bothered" about the traits list and this chapter, consider finding a Christian people-helper. And continue to commit all of this to the Lord.

PRAY: Lord, please help me to be willing—or at least to be willing to be willing—to receive whatever hidden-parts wisdom you want me to know. Teach me to trust you with my past as well as my present and my future. Amen.

Just Ahead

Chapters 3 and 4 focused on how we've been slightly or severely hurt by others, specifically by parents and other adult authority figures. In Chapter 5 we'll discover that in response to those hurts, we developed perceptions and made choices that have hurt us too.

CHAPTER
Five

Hurt by
Childhood Fantasies

I actually remember Saturday morning *radio* programs for children. (Radio is much like T.V. without the pictures and remote control.)

My favorite Saturday morning program, "Let's Pretend," dramatized famous fairy tales like "The Ugly Duckling" and "Sleeping Beauty." Believe me, as a kid in an alcoholic family, I felt like an ugly duckling. What's more, I needed all the Prince-Charming-to-the-rescue fantasies and fairy-tale happy endings I could get!

All of us as young children lived in a fantasyland. Without realizing that we were doing it, we used a kind of magical thinking and fairy-tale logic to make sense of the world around us. If our families were reasonably healthy, we outgrew this thinking as we began to experience the realistic limitations of our magical powers. Unfortunately, all families are not reasonably healthy.

In this chapter we'll examine two of the most influential fantasies young children embrace. We'll also look at what supports these fantasies in childhood and how our lingering childhood fantasies continue to hurt us today.

Childhood Fantasy 1: I Have Unlimited Power to Control

I believe the fantasy of unlimited power to control is the most primitive, powerful, intensely cherished illusion of all individuals—children or adults. The uncut version goes like this: *I have the power to cause events and control other people's behaviors and emotions.*

As young children with limited abilities to correctly interpret our environments, we each saw ourselves as the center of the universe, with the power to cause events and other people's actions. (Come to think of it, I know several mid-lifers who still operate by this principle!)

All children also operate with a kind of fairy-tale logic that good things happen to good people and bad things happen to bad people. Children typically use this let's-pretend perspective to explain why their lives unfold as they do and why people treat them as they do.

This is fine if you are born into a reasonably healthy family led by consistently adequate parents. But this I-have-the-power-to-control-everything-and-everybody fantasy is devastating when you begin life in substantially unhealthy homes. Since no families are perfect and no parents perfectly satisfy their children's every desire, all children to some degree need the second childhood fantasy.

Childhood Fantasy 2:   I Have Unlimited Knowledge to Cure

Let's suppose we discovered as kids that everything and everybody wasn't going exactly the way we wanted and planned. What did we do? We *re*-did! Here's where fantasy number two takes center stage. In its entirety it goes: *If I work hard enough and become good enough, I can make it come out differently next time.*

The "it" we work to make come out differently is a relationship or situation that wounds us visibly or invisibly. Either way, we want to make sure we don't take another blow in the same wounded place. Now this "it" we are dead set on changing might involve making all our unstable families' problems disappear (like the little hero in the cartoon), or something less sweeping like merely curing a parent's alcohol abuse. We just want things to be different next time, even though next time almost always involves the will of another human being. Since we do not have the power to control the will of other humans, this fantasy launches us on hopeless, lifelong quests for next times.

"AND NOW MOM AND DAD, I'LL MAKE
IT DISAPPEAR."

It is as if we are saying to ourselves, "If I can just figure out how to be good enough (smart enough/pretty enough/athletic enough/religious enough/slim enough/wealthy

enough/sexual enough/unsexual enough) I can protect myself
from being abused/unloved/ abandoned.

These fairy-tale fantasies are actually family-perpetuated
myths that help to provide a kind of pathological equilibrium
in unhealthy family systems. Those of us who have been
living by these fantasies have been *mything-out* on a lot of
life. So why do we keep living by them? As we got older, why
didn't they just drop away like dry leaves in autumn?

Reinforcing Childhood Fantasies

When we consider childhood fantasy reinforcers, they seem
to fall into two categories: those all of us encounter about
equally as a natural part of childhood, and those experienced
primarily in hurting and hurtful families—the universal and
the dysfunctional, so to speak. I think we can find two
reinforcers in each category.

Universal Reinforcer 1: Our Own I-dolatry

Playing God is exhausting! I know because I tried it for
years. I did not do a very convincing God imitation, but that
didn't stop me from trying. Even as a dedicated Christian I
approached important relationships from a God-loves-you-
and-Sandy-has-a-wonderful-plan-for-your-life perspective!
As I reflect on that I've-got-to-control-everything-and-every-
body- in-my-life attitude, I've concluded that it is a kind of
I-dolatry, a lust for omnipotence and omniscience.

I think that primarily God is identified by his omnipotence—his unlimited power. So, perhaps our most primitive
and powerful fantasy of omnipotence traces its roots to the
bedrock of original sin and the Tempter's promise that we
could be "like God." If this is true, it is also true that each of
us, in our own turn, re-enacts that Genesis scene as we
wrestle throughout our lives with the primal lust for unlimited power to control our worlds and their inhabitants.

If omnipotence—possessing unlimited power to cause and
control—is the most distinctly god-like attribute of God, then
omniscience runs a close second. Statements such as, "God
knows the end from the beginning," or "God sees around
corners" attempts to grasp the concept of God's omniscience—

his possessing unlimited knowledge about all events and all people for all time.

Undergirding our second fantasy, we discover a lust for figuring out how to change things next time. Of course my determination to know everything about how to fix everything and everybody springs from my desire to control everything and everybody. Again, I think I see the you-will-be-like-God desire rearing its sin-stained head. And we don't have to return to Eden to hear the Tempter's voice.

Universal Reinforcer 2: New Age Spirituality

"Self-empowerment means universal power," according to an article in a magazine published expressly for and about adults raised in hurting and hurtful families.

If we listen closely we'll hear the Eden lie echoing down the corridors of time. This human-beings-have-the-potential-for-unlimited-power message is simply the original tempter's original lie dressed up in a New Age guru's gobbledygook. No wonder it is so popular—it panders to our lust for God's omnipotence and omniscience.

To some degree or another, all of us routinely hear variations on the New Age theme of unlimited human potential. But there are at least two other reinforcers of our childhood fantasies that are not as evenly distributed. They seem to be primarily (although not totally) the domain of unhealthy households.

Dysfunctional Reinforcer 1: Parental Stumbling Blocks

Hang a heavy stone around someone's neck and then drown the person in deep water. That sounds like something from a Mafia handbook, doesn't it? Actually that's Jesus' suggestion for dealing with adults who place stumbling blocks in the paths of children in such a way as to cause those children to stumble. (See Matt. 18:6–7.) Although the context indicates that Jesus' primary emphasis is spiritual, children can be "caused to stumble" in other ways too, because children lack abilities and choices adults have. If I attempted to blame you for causing me to hit you, for example, you would probably conclude I was pretty immature to try to get you to own what belongs to me—personal responsibility for my choices. You would be right. However, if as children we were blamed for Mom's rages, Dad's alcoholism, or maybe even for our own abuse, we did not have the same choice to disbelieve and disregard such blatant attempts to shift an adult's personal responsibility to a child.

The blaming usually sounds something like, "You love to make me hit you, don't you?" Or perhaps the classic, "If you weren't so (whatever), I wouldn't drink so much." Children hear these messages and come to believe, "I cause it by who I am." "It" of course is anything the adult wants to disown.

When we grow up in families where under-responsible, blame-shifting adults run the show, we inevitably gravitate toward another fantasy reinforcer.

Dysfunctional Reinforcer 2:   Need for Self-protection

As children in hurtful families, we needed the fantasies spun by our childish, magical thinking to keep us from drowning in the endless horror of utter helplessness. As painful as it was to believe we were so rotten and worthless that we caused our perfectly nice parents to neglect or abuse us, there is something far worse. It is the desolate terror of acknowledging that *our parents made their own hurtful choices about how to treat us and we were completely powerless to stop them.*

Think about how fragile you were as a little child. Can you imagine how overwhelmingly terrifying it would have been to have faced and felt your utter defenselessness? No wonder children in hurtful homes need the protective fantasy of omnipotence and omniscience provided by believing, "If I caused it (hands-on or hands-off abuse), then I can control whether or not it happens."

The more chaotic and out-of-control our families felt to us as children, the greater our determination to become more skillful controllers. We can focus our attention on controlling externals—people and circumstances, or on controlling internals—our emotions, thoughts, and memories. Most of us focus on both.

The problem with fantasies, fairy tales, and myths is that they bear a strong resemblance to one of the stories I used to hear on "Let's Pretend" about the emperor's new clothes. Trying to protect ourselves with fantasies is like trying to keep warm in a snowstorm wearing only what the emperor wore. His new clothes weren't real; neither are our fantasies. But they sure are powerful. And persistent.

If my line of reasoning is correct, we would expect to see the effects of these fantasies in our adult lives. I believe that we do. I also believe that the deeper our wounds from childhood, the more likely we are to base our lives today on self-protective fantasies.

To some degree, *all our adult relationships are family reunions.* Usually we scan our environments searching for people who resemble our earliest and most significant others—our folks or other important adults from our childhood, such as an incest perpetrator. Each of these family-reunion style relationships offers us another opportunity to remake the original childhood interactions come out with a happier ending.

For example, when they still operate from a combination of fantasies one and two, adult incest survivors often wear loose—even baggy—clothing that conceals the contours of their bodies. They still believe that the shape of their bodies caused that perfectly nice person to molest them, so they will make interactions with potential perpetrators come out differently this time by hiding their shapes.

However, these same, shapelessly clothed incest survivors may screen out awareness of sexually unsafe situations that make them sitting ducks for rape and other forms of sexual abuse. That's the problem with self-protective fantasies. They don't keep us any safer than the child's empty deodorant container with the label guaranteeing 100 percent protection. Many of us see painful and baffling similarities in all our adult relationships because we are relating out of unrecognized fantasies.

The words *fairy-tale fantasies* sound so harmless, don't they? They sort of conjure up scenes of Tinkerbell and Peter

Pan. The tragic truth is that childhood fantasies can have unbearably painful, life-changing effects.

Karen's Story:
The Tragedy of Living a Childhood Fantasy

As you can imagine, I've heard many heart-breaking, gut-twisting examples of childhood pain over the years as a Bible teacher and informal people-helper and then as a counselor and conference speaker. But few compare with Karen's story.

Karen is one of the most stunningly attractive young women you could ever meet. She is happily married, a devoted mom, and a deeply committed Christian who works hard in counseling to correct all the distorted thinking she learned as a child in a very hurting and hurtful family.

Karen's dad worked in Middle-Eastern oil fields, which took him away from the family for long stretches of time. That's difficult enough to handle when you're a kid. But it's even harder if you have a mother who is a schizophrenic of the I-am-Cleopatra-queen-of-the-Nile variety. Karen's mom was. So Karen and her older brother and younger sister often got shuttled to this aunt or that grandparent during Mother's frequent psychiatric hospitalizations.

Even when her mom was at home, Karen was neither safe nor secure. In fact, the most tragic event of her childhood occurred during one of her mother's at-home times. This is how Karen described it to me.

"The summer I was five, the elderly man across the street molested me several times in his basement. I remember one time his wife even came down and saw what he was doing. I thought she'd help me and make him quit, but she didn't say or do anything. I didn't understand exactly what was happening. But I knew it was wrong and I really, really wanted it to stop.

"Somehow I think I tried to tell my mother so she would make him quit. I should have known better because she fell apart, of course. I remember her yelling and screaming as she scrubbed me in the bathtub. She scrubbed and scrubbed so hard I thought my skin would come off. She called me 'bad' and 'a dirty little girl.' And she told me God couldn't love bad, dirty little girls."

Up to this point Karen had told her story in a calm, emotionless voice. But her tone dropped, her voice cracked, and she began to weep softly.

"I just knew that what he [the perpetrator] did made me filthy, and because I was a bad, dirty little girl my mommy and God couldn't love me. Somehow I had to get rid of him [the perpetrator] and make myself clean enough and good enough to be loved."

Karen sobbed convulsively as she repeatedly attempted to continue. "So I—I began to . . ."

Again Karen's crying silenced her. She finished the story with many pauses to sob, catch her breath, and blow her nose.

Karen described to me in detail how she began to insert her entire, small-boned, five-year-old hand—up to her wrist—into her anus to gouge and rip-out layer after layer of anal and rectal tissue in an attempt to "get rid of him" and cleanse her body from the filth of the sexual abuse! She did that over and over again as she sat on the toilet or in the bathtub until the water in each ran red with her blood and bloody chunks of her body.

"One time my little sister came in and screamed when she saw me sitting in blood-red bath water. She ran and called my mom, who came in, looked at it, and said, 'Oh she'll be all right.' Then she turned around and left the room.

"I hate myself for what I did to my body—how I hurt myself. I've always been afraid of God's anger at me for what I did to myself, especially now."

Karen's "now" included a probable colostomy due to irreparable damage to her body. A specialist told Karen that because of multiple layers of scar tissue, her anal opening was the diameter of a pencil.

Clearly Karen's childhood fantasy of "I can make it come out different next time by making myself good and clean enough to earn Mommy's and God's love" altered her life tragically because of the method she chose. In counseling, Karen came to see herself for the first time as the young, helpless, cognitively limited little girl she was when she was sexually abused. She realized how logical her choice had been from a child's perspective.

I invited Karen to enter, in her imagination, the bathroom where that little girl sat in bloody bathwater after having been emotionally abandoned by her mentally disturbed mother. I asked her to do and say what that desolate child, she herself, needed at that desperate moment. Karen wept as she told her child-self the truth she had needed to hear for so many years:

"You didn't cause it, and it wasn't your fault."

"God has always loved you, and he always will."

"God is angry about what the abuser did to your body; he is not angry about what you did to your body because he understands that you did the best you knew to do as a little child."

"You are a very brave little girl, and I am *so* sorry you were hurt so badly."

Few of us will have such devastating proof of the power of childhood fantasies. Yet all of us must come to recognize their impact on our hurting and hurtful ways if we want to realize the promise of healing.

Pause to Ponder and Pray

PONDER: Read the following statements and check the ones that describe your views:

___ If I were a better person (or better Christian), I could change my spouse/child/friend/other.

___ If someone disagrees with me, his or her opinions are almost always right.

___ I am responsible for my family's/my office's/my Bible study's/other's problems.

___ When things go wrong, it's usually my fault.

___ If I (whatever), then (whoever) would (whatever). For example, if I would start sleeping with my boyfriend as he wants me to, then he would not read so much pornography or threaten to date other women.

All of the above statements reveal the influence of childhood fantasies.

More truth-based perceptions include:

✔ I do not have the power to change anyone no matter how much "better" I get.

✔ My opinions are apt to be as valid as anyone else's opinions.

✔ I share responsibility for the atmosphere of my family/office/Bible study/other.

✔ When things go wrong, I sometimes own a degree of responsibility, and sometimes I don't.

✔ My boyfriend is totally responsible for choosing his behaviors.

PRAY: Lord, please help me to trust you enough to let you be who you, and *you alone*, are—the Event Controller and People Changer. Thank you for understanding how difficult that is for me when I consider some of the deeply wounding circumstances you have allowed into my life. Amen.

Just Ahead

In the next chapter, we look at two life-dominating choices we made as youngsters living in the "Let's Pretend" fantasyland of childhood.

CHAPTER
Six

Hurt by
Childhood Choices

In great measure, our lives equal the sum of our choices.

As I've already said, I believe our earliest, most basic choice is: *Stay alive.* If that's true, then all of our subsequent decisions are founded upon, structured by, and supportive of that primal, life-affirming choice. Although who we are today is the result of thousands of choices made over decades of living, I think the vast majority of those decisions were based upon, and guided by, our responses to three questions every human being must answer repeatedly from the moment of birth:

> Can I be safe?
> Can I be me?
> Can I be accepted?

Our earliest responses to these questions become fountainhead decisions from which flow the spiritual, personal, and relational patterns of our lives. All of us had to begin making these three life-shaping responses as very young, easily confused (perhaps even abused) children lacking the cognitive development necessary to accurately interpret the events going on around us!

It's not surprising that many of us have hurt ourselves and others as we've lived out these early childhood choices. Let's examine the three universal early childhood choice points and identify our life-shaping responses.

Childhood Choice 1: Can I Be Safe?

This first question, or choice point, speaks to the issue of trust. Each of us made this and all of our early choices based on our perceptions and conclusions about whether or not our newborn universes—our families—were safe places where our deep, life-affirming longings would be met by consistently competent, caring authority figures.

If our homes were reasonably healthy and stable, we likely concluded that we could depend on our parents and other adults to recognize and meet our needs. We sensed that we could trust them to take care of us and keep us safe, until we got bigger and could be personally responsible for our own safety.

Of course, our perceptions about our parents and other significant adult caregivers carried over to our concepts of our heavenly Parent. This means that if we had consistently competent, trustworthy parents, we were apt to conclude that God also could be trusted to know and meet our needs, care for us, and keep us safe. As we got older and more theologically sophisticated, we realized that our trustworthy, loving God never promised to keep us pain-*free* or immune from the blows of an unsafe world. So we had to learn how to balance the truth of God's constant care with the reality of life's unceasing uncertainties and relentless risks.

In contrast, if we were born into unstable households, we probably concluded very early that we had to figure out how to keep ourselves safe, since none of the bigger people—mothers and fathers—could be trusted to take care of us in a way that felt genuinely safe.

God likely got "tarred with the same brush" as our parents. If so, we assumed that the heavenly Parent could not be trusted to keep us safe, either. Besides, if God really is in charge of everything (as we may have heard in church or elsewhere), then God is responsible for sticking us with such unstable and unsafe parents.

In effect, this choice says, "My folks cannot be trusted to keep me safe. If there is a God, I cannot trust that God to meet my deep needs and keep me safe, either. (After all, basic safety is a very deep need.) Therefore I will trust only myself to get my needs met and to stay safe.

Answering this basic who-can-I-trust-to-keep-me-safe question is arguably the most important issue of life, and it is inextricably bound to will-I-choose-to-stay-alive? When as babies or very young children we sensed the lack of safety in our unstable, hurtful homes, we naturally and self-protectively began looking to ourselves to restructure our environments in a way that would keep us safe enough to stay alive. In so doing, we prolonged the normal "magical thinking" of childhood by keeping ourselves at the center of our personal universes.

Obviously, when all our trust and safety "eggs" are in *our* baskets, everything in life centers on us! That's why our responses to the second must-answer question are so significant.

Childhood Choice 2: Can I Be Me?

This choice embodies show-and-tell at its most nitty-gritty level. The basic issue is whether or not it is safe within our families to recognize and express our authentic, human—sometimes messy and unpleasant—needs and feelings and all the other elements of our real, human selves—flaws included. If it is safe, we usually resolve to know ourselves and show ourselves as honestly as possible.

We transfer that attitude to our relationships with God by believing that he wants us to be honest with him about our real feelings and needs. After all, God knows us far better than we will ever know ourselves, and he loves us still.

In hurting and hurtful families, however, we learned soon after birth that it was not safe to put our core identities on the line. If we did reveal our natural, normal neediness and vulnerability, our folks may have withdrawn emotionally, attacked brutally, or—more likely—exhibited some mixture of both responses. However they chose to convey their message, "You aren't allowed to have needs and feelings because ours already absorb all our energy and interests," we heard it loud and clear.

Many of us determined that the best way to meet our needs was to eliminate our needs. It hurt too much to recognize and reveal needs time after time without getting them met. The problem is that denying needs and deadening feelings does not make them disappear. They merely go underground to pop up later in surprising and often hurtful disguises.

The reasoning behind this choice to conceal our genuine needs and emotions goes something like this: "Obviously, just being myself and expressing my real needs is going to bring emotional (and sometimes even physical) pain. I seem to be a huge disappointment and a colossal burden to the big people who are supposed to take care of me. I'd better learn how to hide my true self and my true struggles or I won't survive."

What's worse, *our real needs and feelings are major components of what makes us who we are.* So the logical conclusion for a child is something like: "I must be bad the way I am—the way I really am. To keep myself safe, I must not show the real me with all my neediness, my vulnerability to being emotionally and relationally wounded, and my imperfections. The safest way to keep from accidentally showing the real me is to avoid knowing the real me. So I will stop tuning in to my genuine longings and emotions. Yeah, that will work. No genuine personal needs. No real human feelings or flaws. That's the ticket."

Clearly as young children we lacked the psychological sophistication to knowingly reason our ways through the mazes of our perceptions to reach the conclusions spelled out above. Clearly, too, the amount of hurting in our families directly affected the intensity with which we continued to choose to mask our identities and hide our imperfections. But no matter how heavy our identity masks became, we usually kept dragging them along as we limped through life. After all, the alternative—being seen for who we are and being deemed unacceptable—was worse.

Childhood Choice 3: Can I Be Accepted?

We do not just have relationships. At the core of our very beings, we are relational. This reality illuminates the unutterable intensity of our need to be accepted and found eligible for relationships—in a word, *loved.* So, the third crucial question asks: How do I qualify for what psychology and sociology folks might call "relational attachment," more commonly known as acceptance and love? Again, we answered with choices born soon after we were.

Ideally parents love their children for no other reason than that they are their children. That certainly is the biblical model. God sovereignly chose to set his love upon us when there was nothing whatsoever lovable about us. (See Rom. 5:8.) In other words, our love relationship with God began totally one-sided. But ideally it doesn't end there.

Scripture says that when we choose to love God we do so "because he first loved us." (See 1 John 4:19.) In effect the loved become lovers. That's usually true in human families, too. Most children who are secure in their parents' love will develop loving natures which they express through their own unique personalities.

In contrast to this secure and settled sense of being loved just for themselves—flaws and all—children raised by impaired, shame-bound parents are apt to have a very different mental monologue playing. Here's how it may sound: "Just being me isn't good enough to get my folks' approval and love. They seem to accept me more the harder I work to please them. I never quite seem to be good enough to earn their full acceptance and love. But if I keep trying to figure out how to perform and please them perfectly enough, maybe *someday* I'll earn their seal of approval and the gift of their love.

"God, the heavenly Father, must also love me more when I do more religious performing. Since I'm not ever sure that

I really please God, I'll just keep trying to work hard enough and be good enough to earn his grace and love."

Let's summarize the choice options we had in response to the three basic and universal questions we must all answer. The chart below displays the questions, the issues each addresses, and the choices we were apt to make depending on the relative health of our birth families. And it includes a life statement capsulizing the relational patterns produced by our contrasting basic choices.

Primary Choice of All Children: Stay Alive

Spiritual Arena of Trust Issues (Universal Question: Can I Be Safe?)	
In Safe, Secure, Stable Family	In Unsafe, Insecure, Unstable Family
Child's Basic Choice: I will trust my folks to keep me safe now. I will trust myself to keep me safe when I am bigger. I will trust God to keep me safe always.	Child's Basic Choice: I will trust only myself, now and always.

Personal Arena of Identity Issues (Universal Question: Can I Be Me?)	
In Safe, Secure, Stable Family	In Unsafe, Insecure, Unstable Family
Child's Basic Choice: I will know and show who I really am.	Child's Basic Choice: I will hide who I really am from myself and from others.

Relational Arena of Attachment Issues (Universal Question: Can I Be Accepted?)	
In Safe, Secure, Stable Family	In Unsafe, Insecure, Unstable Family
Child's Basic Choice: I will accept myself since I am accepted by those who love me.	Child's Basic Choice: I will try hard to be good enough to earn acceptance and to be loved.

Summary of Contrasting Childhood Choices

Child from Consistently Stable Family	Child from Consistently Unstable Family
I will trust trustworthy people and God. I can be, know, and develop because I am accepted for myself in real love relationships.	I will trust myself to stay safe by hiding the real me from myself and others. I'll try to please so I can be good enough to earn acceptance and love.

Which of these basic choice patterns seems more familiar? If it is the second, the earn acceptance pattern, I certainly can relate.

My Childhood Choices Legacy

I was launched into a performance-oriented lifestyle at least by the age of five, if not before. You see, I began piano lessons shortly before my fifth birthday and was playing in public at churches and community gatherings within a few months. Some of my earliest memories feature my mother's smiling face as she basked in the glow of compliments about her talented little daughter. I wasn't really all that great, but Phoenix was a small place half-a-century ago, and there was a severe shortage of homegrown five-year-old pianists!

Like any little kid, I lapped up all that attention and approval. My dad (stepdad really, but I didn't know that until age ten) was away in World War II. My mom worked all day at the hospital, and often spent the evenings down-town packing parachutes. The elderly couple from whom we rented a room cared for me adequately but in an unemotional, spartan fashion.

But there was something else. I distinctly remember feeling more secure and acceptable when I earned my mother's smile and made her feel happy and proud. She really did seem to be happiest when others complimented her. Oh, I knew my mother loved me because she told me she did. I just seemed to be safer somehow when Mother was pleased and proud about something I had done.

My mother had decided years before to earn acceptance in her family and in life by being good enough, smart enough, helpful enough, and whatever else enough it took. It was only natural for my mother to teach me a pain-born and pain-filled keep-myself-safe-by-hiding-the-real-me-while-pleasing-and-performing-to-earn-acceptance lifestyle. And believe me, I was a fast learner!

This is how our life-shaping childhood choices were shaped by our parents' life-shaping childhood choices, which, in turn, were shaped by the generation before, and so on. And whatever the circumstances, because of normal developmental limitations, children have no choice except to receive everything parents and other adults tell them as Truth with a capital *T*. This is the primary reason little children can be caused to stumble so easily. Here's a closer look at the subject of childhood stumbling I introduced earlier.

Childhood Stumbling and Childhood Choices

I suggested in the previous chapter that Jesus' words in Matthew 18:6 could have more than a spiritual application. The word translated *stumble* in the King James version of this passage (and *sin* in other versions) paints a word picture of how parents and other adults can cause children to trip and fall over obstacles of false teaching placed directly in the children's paths.[1]

Children always believe that adults know everything about everything and always tell the truth about everything. This natural, but naive and erroneous, assumption empowers adults to create children's universes and cause those children to stumble into distorted and hurtful patterns of thinking and choosing. Let me illustrate.

I grew up in an English-speaking universe since I was born into an English-speaking family. It is like being a worm in an apple, I suppose. To the worm, the apple is the entire universe!

Living in an English-speaking universe meant I didn't know other languages existed. I couldn't wake up one morning and suddenly choose to begin thinking and speaking in French or Italian. Literally I had no choice but to think and speak in English—my parents' language—for without at least two options from which to select, we don't have a genuine choice.

Suppose that when I got older I noticed that some families did not always—or ever—use English and I asked my folks to explain. They might have told me that I was stupid (or crazy) for even thinking about the possibility of using another language. They might even have made veiled threats of emotional abandonment with statements such as, "No kid of ours is going to go around speaking some strange, foreign language!"

On some deep, life-preserving level of my inner person, I would have heard the implication that I was disloyal to even raise the language issue. I'd know that if I wanted to stay a secure, firmly attached part of their family, I had better learn to think and speak their way and only their way. Having no alternative source of food, shelter, relationship, and the other life-sustaining elements my family provided, I would have had no choice but to adopt my parents' representations of reality, including their perspectives on acceptable language.

Without recognizing my self-protective choice, I would have embraced my parents' English-only perceptual grid as the one, true, morally upright (perhaps even "biblically orthodox") world view. What's more, I would have believed that I chose it freely, when in fact, I had no other option except emotional orphaning.

I would have subsequently sifted every experience, inside or outside of the family, through that perceptual grid. These die-hard, parent-powered interpretive filters come with lifetime warranties, you know. (Indeed, some of you *do* know!) To maintain my loyal-child status, thereby avoiding the pain of my parents' emotional abandonment, I would have continued to automatically exclude other language choices—even as an adult.

Adult Pain from Childhood Choices

Tragically many of us continue to live out our early childhood choices year after pain-filled year of our adult lives as if we have no more options now than we had as parent-dependent youngsters. But we do!

When we were young children, our parents and other adults had the power to control us by controlling the way they presented reality to us. As we became adults, they no longer automatically possessed that power unless we ceded it to them. This means that, while our parents will always influence us, they cannot control us today without our full participation in that *childifying* process.

Somewhere on our journeys to adulthood, many of us chose to continue relating to our parents as if we were still young children without the options of independent thought and volition. When we do that, we are choosing to grow *down* instead of grow *up*. And here's the tricky part about this whole self-childification mess: We usually don't have a clue that we're making such a decision! However, continuing to structure our lives based on choices made in early childhood inevitably contributes to our hurting and hurtful ways.

Pause to Ponder and Pray

PONDER: Re-read the chart summarizing the basic choices we may have made in early childhood in response to the three universal issues of trust, identity, and attachment. Then answer the following questions.

✔ Do I tend to "overtrust" by automatically assuming that everyone is trustworthy?

✔ Do I tend to "undertrust" by continually distrusting people who have demonstrated their consistent (but imperfect) trustworthiness?

✔ On a scale of 1 to 10, how well do I know myself? (1 = clueless; 10 = totally)

✔ On a scale of 1 to 10, how well do I accept myself? (1 = no way; 10 = totally)

In 25 words or less, write your capsule life choices statement. Be sure to include a phrase addressing trust, identity, and attachment issues like the summary statements in the chart.

PRAY: Lord, please help me see how I have used your awesome gift of choice to protect myself as a child. Please show me the ways in which my childhood choices hurt me and those I love today. And thank you for being so patient with me as I fear and falter in this scary process of letting you give me wisdom in my hidden parts. Amen.

Just Ahead

It's very hard work to significantly alter lifetime patterns. But we can do it. And there's no doubt that we'll meet with some resistance when we dare to reclaim the privilege of choice we may have relinquished years ago. But it's worth all the hard work and all the flak we'll get along the way.

So if you're feeling excited, apprehensive, eager, confused, or terrified, read on. It sounds like you're all set to get really serious about this healing, mending, and changing business.

CHAPTER
Seven

Help for
Healing Our Hurts

Most of our adult life problems were our childhood solutions.

Our naturally self-protective childhood solutions expressed our childhood perceptions and choices. Our childhood choices were very limited. So it isn't surprising that our childhood solutions, extended into adulthood, have proved very limiting. This principle of childhood solutions becoming adult life problems is seen clearly and dramatically in the lives of those adults who have multiple personality disorder, M.P.D.

A Dramatic Example: M.P.D.

As children, multiples employed their God-given abilities to disconnect from unbearable trauma by creating mental companions to help them bear it. Barriers of amnesia usually separate these mental companions, which means that often one inner part knows nothing of the other parts. We don't have to be experts in multiple personality disorder to deduce that this sanity-saving blessing of childhood becomes a confusion-causing problem in adult life.

I have counseled with multiples who frequently and skillfully fake knowing someone or something that should be well known to them but isn't. In reality, the unremembered friend or fact is well known to the multiple. Well known, that is, to a different part of the multiple than the part who is in charge at the awkward friend-meeting or fact-needing moment. Actually, this is a tame example of the confusing, painful adult life effects of multiplicity. Since most of us do not have multiple personality disorder, we may miss the more subtle manifestations of this principle in our lives. I know. For a long time I did.

A More Subtle Example: Me

As a youngster I decided to solve the problem of my mother's overworked, under-loved, single-parent sadness by performing as well as possible as often as possible to earn compliments for her, and to earn acceptance and a greater sense of personal safety for me. That solution seemed to work so well, I used it over and over.

By the time I was an adult, I had become a world-class performer and pleaser. In fact, in many ways, I became my self-protective solution! As a result, I directed most of my energy to polishing my performances rather than developing my character. This external emphasis caused a lot of problems for me and for those dearest to me.

Whether we are multiples, perfectionistic performers and pleasers, or hurting and hurtful in some other way, we have one thing in common. A long time ago we had a scary and painful problem; we chose the best solution we could at the time, but it isn't working anymore. Our solutions have become our problems. Clearly, something's got to change!

This chapter is about change. In the next few pages we'll explore a practical plan for change, the problems and pain of change, and the power source for change. As we do, we'll turn the corner, from understanding how we became hurting and hurtful people to looking at how we can become healing and helpful people. Wouldn't that be a change!

Some Preliminaries to Change

Where do we typically focus when we want to change? Our adult lifestyles and relationships, right? That's only natural. But our adult lives, with their hurting and hurtful ways, are the composites of earlier and repeated choices. Here's what I mean: *What we live with, we learn, and what we learn, we practice. What we practice, we become, and what we become has consequences.*[1]

Re-stating that sequence may clarify it:

1. What we lived with,
2. What we learned,
3. What we've practiced and continue practicing,
4. What we've become (meaning the prevailing patterns of our lives), and
5. The past and present consequences of those life-patterns.

Whether it's formal and expensive with a therapist in an office or informal and *gratis* with a friend over coffee, most folks seek counseling because of painful consequences from their prevailing life patterns, that is, "number five pain" using the sequence above. That's why I went. And I've noticed that many of us sincere change-seekers look for someone or something that will help us get new and different consequences from our old familiar choices.

To use the well-worn roots/fruits analogy, we run around lopping off our adult life "fruits"—expecting an entirely new species to grow—without giving any thought to checking their roots. That is, we expect number five to suddenly be different while numbers one through four remain the same. When we think of it that way, this expectation not only sounds unrealistic, it sounds absurd!

If we want genuine, gut-level changes in the fruits of our lives, we must uncover, identify, and tear out the poisonous roots of deception while we sow new seeds of life-giving truth in their places. If we want new consequences, we must make new choices. And if we do, our lives will change.

Wilson's Theory of Change

For several years in conferences and seminary classes I've been discussing my theory about what produces change in our lives. It's not very complex or particularly elegant, but I think it covers the basics. Wilson's Theory of Change says: *Making and consistently practicing new choices produces change.* In other words:

NEW CHOICES + CONSISTENT PRACTICE = CHANGE

Owning Our Choices

Have you ever stopped to consider that we cannot *change* what we did not *choose?* We confront that reality with blood, sweat, toil, and tears when we work in vain to change other people's choices. Perhaps even more germane to our immediate discussion: *We won't know we can change what we don't know we have chosen.* This means that recognizing and intentionally reclaiming, or owning, our choices is a mandatory prerequisite to changing those choices.

This process of reviewing childhood perceptions and choices seems to fit into our putting-away-childish-things assignment mentioned in 1 Corinthians 13:11. In that verse, the apostle Paul told a group of struggling—dare I say, hurting and hurtful—first century Christians that becoming mature includes putting away childish things.

How would the apostle Paul, those Corinthian Christians, you, I, or anyone else know what parts of our belief systems were "childish things" unless we reviewed and reevaluated our childhood perceptions and choices from a more mature, hopefully wiser, perspective? When we were children, everything we believed may have *been* childish, but nothing we believed would have *seemed* childish. What we believed just was. And that hook-line-and-sinker swallowing of our family-shaped realities as ultimate reality makes this putting-away-childish-things enterprise quite a challenge.

Pastor and counselor David Seamands helps us understand this when he says, "Childish things don't simply fall away by themselves as dead leaves fall from a tree. We have to put them away, *katargeo* them, and be 'finished with childish things.' "[2]

The strong Greek verb *katargeo* means "to abolish, wipe out, [or] set aside something."[3] Those phrases picture a powerful, purposeful, energetic endeavor, not an automatic or casual occurrence. We may automatically outgrow measles, mumps, or acne. But childhood misperceptions must be purposefully set aside and replaced with accurate understanding.

So much for the preliminaries to change. We're ready to proceed to the heart of our change plan as it's presented in the chart found on the following page.

The change-plan chart visually displays the elements and process involved in change. Look at each element, noticing specifically which can be changed and which cannot.

<u>Cannot-Change Elements</u>

The first dotted rectangle (moving left to right) is different from the others for two reasons. First, it is the only rectangle divided into two sections. Second, it is the only one representing elements that are beyond the grasp of our new choices; therefore, these elements cannot be changed. These fixed elements include:

- Our parents' sin natures
- Our parents' genetic predispositions, such as susceptibility to alcoholism or schizophrenia, and natural endowments, such as level of intelligence
- Our parents' personal issues, such as routine responsibilities or life-dominating problems
- Our parents' attitudes and actions toward us
- Family atmosphere, that is, how safe and stable
- Our own sin natures
- Our own genetic predispositions and natural endowments

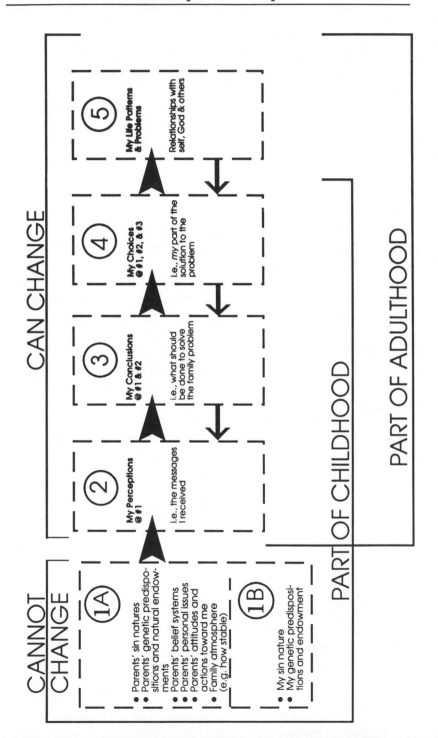

There really are some unchangeable components in our lives. We must remember that no matter how much we'd like to be taller or shorter, for example, we cannot really change our height. At best we can modify it only slightly. And as much as we long to have had two adoring parents and a stable birth family, some of us never did and never will. Nevertheless, in comparison to the unchangeables, we have many more elements in our lives open to new choices and changes.

Elements We Can Change

Look again at the change-plan chart and you'll notice that three of the elements exist as parts of both childhood and adult life: early perceptions, conclusions, and choices. A fourth element, represented by dotted rectangle number 5, belongs exclusively to our adult lives. It is also the sum, in large part, of everything depicted by rectangles 1 through 4.

We must be willing to identify and reevaluate our childhood fantasies (perceptions and conclusions) and our childhood choices so that we will better understand our present manner of living. That reviewing process gives us a more complete context in which to make new choices. Let's take one hypothetical situation that illustrates this process.

If our parents were too distracted by their own unacknowledged, life-dominating problems and pain to be appropriately nurturing, we learned to discount and deny our natural needs and normal feelings. In effect our folks sent this message: "I can't take it when you have needs or make requests or demands." In response most likely our life-affirming, self-protective choice was: "I won't ever have any need for nurturing. That way my folks won't be upset and overwhelmed. And that way I won't have to face how really unavailable and inadequate they are."

Then painfully and paradoxically, the child begins to take care of the parents by appearing to have no needs, so that the parents can appear to take care of the child! The next table is a summary of this example and the part of the process it illustrates.

Parents' Issues and Family Atmosphere	Child's Perceptions	Child's Conclusion
Significantly impaired parents and unsafe, insecure family atmosphere	I will not stay alive without my parents' care, but my parents get upset and are not there for me when I need care.	I will have to protect and take care of my parents, i.e., fix them, so they will be able to protect and take care of me.

Keeping in mind that children have developmentally limited reasoning abilities, what might children in such situations choose to do to keep themselves alive? These are some possibilities:

- *I will have no needs.* (Reasoning: My needs are bad because my needs overwhelm my parents and then they are even less able to care for me and keep me safe.)

- *I will have no feelings.* (Reasoning: Feelings are dangerous because my parents can't tolerate my feelings without getting overwhelmed.)

- *I will try hard to require no care from my parents and to be good enough to make my parents want to care for me and keep me safe.* (Reasoning: When I make my needs known, my parents aren't able to care for me, so I get my needs met by not having any needs of my own and by trying to meet theirs.)

Probable Adult Life Patterns

"If we don't change our direction, we are apt to end up where we are headed," says an ancient Chinese proverb. With that timeless truth in view, let's consider this question: What might our adult life relational patterns be if we never changed our direction, that is, if we continued to live and relate based on childhood perceptions, conclusions, and choices in our example? These are some probable outcomes:

- *In our relationships with God:* We would be prone to believe we earn our right standing with God by doing as much as possible *for* him while asking as little as possible *from* him.

- *In our relationships with others:* It's likely we would maximize the care-taking skills we honed by parenting such impaired and childified parents as those in our example. Relatively healthy, well-functioning people wouldn't interest us much, because—as we might be overheard saying—"they don't really need me." And we would *need* to be needed to feel really comfortable in relationships.

- *In our relationships with ourselves:* When we're devoting so much time and energy to taking care of others, there's not enough left over to take appropriate care of ourselves. Besides if we grew up in homes like those in our example, we learned that we were from a remarkable, mutant strain of humans who were born without personal needs.

If we continued living out these probable adult life consequences of the probable childhood choices described in our illustration, we would eventually burn out or break down from exhaustion—physical, emotional, and spiritual. At least, let's hope so, because we rarely seek change until the alternative is even worse!

The Change Plan in Action: Karen

Remember Karen, who ripped out her own flesh in her heartbreaking quest to be good and clean enough to get Mommy and God to love her? Karen did not begin to heal emotionally and spiritually until she revisited and reviewed—looked again at—her desperate childhood choices. Karen raged and wept as she confronted the truth about the emotionally impoverished, chaotic, dangerous home life created by her parents' physical and emotional abandonment.

Only then could she begin to accept God's love and believe he was not angry because of what she did to her body. Only then could Karen start to genuinely forgive her parents. Only then could she stop hating and start forgiving that "stupid little girl" who literally tore herself apart to make herself lovable. And only then, at long last, could that desperate little girl find peace.

In counseling, Karen worked at consistently practicing new choices of how to think about and relate to herself and

others. She learned to set appropriate boundaries and respect her own needs as she worked hard, wept often, and went
on working. Today Karen would tell you that the freeing,
healing truth she's gained is worth the high price of change.

The Price of Change

Hidden hurts. Suffocating secrets. Like weeds, they grow
relentlessly through the cracks in our souls, threatening to
overrun our lives. Why would we hesitate a millisecond to
acknowledge and uncover them no matter what the cost?
Many of us fear the light of truth that reveals them, for truth
brings suffering as well as freedom.

We must enter the change process with open eyes. When
we do, we'll see that the necessary truth necessarily requires
tears, time, and even some terror. Tears? Of course, because
change is an excruciating blend of losses as well as gains.
Time? Indeed, since quick fixes work only in fantasyland.
Some terror? You bet. Letting go of old ways before we firmly
grasp the new is nothing less than terrifying.   And woven
throughout the tears, time, and terror, we see truth, truth
again, and more truth.

Tears About Family Losses as a Price of Change

I doubt we can ever put our pasts *behind* us when we've
never put them *before* us. Yet many of us stall on the starting
line of change because we fear that we'll lose family members'
approval and affection.

I once counseled with a charming thirty-something Christian who grew up in a subtly, but profoundly, unhealthy
home. She said her birth family's motto was "family first." I
think that meant, "Ignore and don't talk about who and
what's hurtful in this family." An alternative translation
might be: "Don't rock the boat (with truth) even if it's the
Titanic!"

We will never begin the move from hurting to healing until
we answer the question: "Whose rules rule?" The person
whose rules we are living by is god to us! If, in an attempt to
gain the parental seal of approval, we continue to live by the
rules of hurting, hurtful parents, we will continue our hurt-

ing, hurtful ways. But if we choose to know God and put him on the throne of our lives, we will begin to live by his rules. And, as we've already seen, God takes truth very seriously.

I read somewhere that calling a thing by its correct name is the beginning of change. Some of us will need to begin calling our family loyalty *lying,* if that is its correct name. Yet, just contemplating such a genuinely truth-based approach to our entire lives, we may feel as alien in our families as salmon would be in the Sahara! Yet God and commitment to change call us to begin dealing honestly with our pasts as well as our present lives. We must face the pain inherent in becoming truth-tellers in truth-fearing families. We are foolish to expect reality-phobic family members to jump up, click their heels together, and exclaim, "Oh, goody goody. We've all been wondering when someone would get healthy enough to start changing so that we'd be confronted with our personal and family dysfunction and be dragged kicking and screaming into greater wholeness!" It just doesn't work that way.

In unhealthy systems, whether they're families or companies, the person who sees and speaks the problem becomes the problem. Instead of working to resolve the problem, such systems focus on removing the problem-perceiver.

Truth About Blaming as a Price of Change

I've made much of the fact that children do not have the same choices adults have because of their limited cognitive abilities. I've described at length how as children we were caused to stumble into distorted thinking and choosing patterns. I believe all of this is true. But, now that we are adults, I believe this is not all that is true. Some of us must face the truth that we have gotten bogged-down in blaming our parents or other powerful people in our childhoods.

Sincerely struggling changers usually detour only temporarily onto a parent-blaming track. Sadly, a few folks homestead there. They find support in books, usually written by therapists, who tell them things like "forgiving parents is for wimps."[4] That approach may sell books or attract counseling clients, but I don't think it is genuinely helpful. And clearly it is not biblical.

Ezekiel 18:20 says that each of us dies [experiences the consequences] for our own sins. Not fathers dying for children's sins, nor children for fathers'. But all for their own. Even more pertinent to our "caused to stumble" discussion, Ezekiel 18:30 tells us to repent and turn away from all our sins so that they "may not become a stumbling block" to us (NASB). Clearly there is a transfer of primary responsibility in the stumbling block department when we become adults. Said differently, *we must each take responsibility for our own choices.*

One of our most important choices will be to invest the time necessary to underwrite the cost of genuine change.

Time as a Price of Change

So many of us hurting Christians sincerely search for an anointed amnesia with a lifetime guarantee. We think (and may have been taught) that all memories of unpleasant facts and all manifestations of unpleasant feelings are instantly, totally erased at the moment of salvation. Let's face it, we want an evangelical zap! And if we don't get that, the next best thing is for God to meet our demands for magical makeovers.

"Process" is an obscene concept for many of us raised in unhealthy families. In fact, I sometimes joke about process being the P word. Schooled in dichotomous all-or-nothing concepts, we learned that on a scale of one to ten, there are only two possibilities. One. Or ten. This way or that way, period. Consequently, we usually think only in terms of extreme polarities: wrong or right, bad or good. Or, more pertinent to our ongoing focus, wounded or well, hurt or healed.

We risk sabotaging our own change adventures when we forget to take a process perspective. Said differently, change takes not only tears, but time. More accurately, change takes a lifetime! Maybe you know people who undertake a thirty-day miracle makeover. Or perhaps you know others who commit to a slightly more realistic six-month recovery program.

I think Scripture presents the most helpful and realistic plan. It's called *mind renewal,* and it appears to span a lifetime. (See Rom. 12:2.) After all, the Israelites spent a full generation conquering enemies after God took them into the promised land. Don't you think God was every bit as much in that generation-long conquering process as he was in the bringing-them-in event? And what about Moses' forty years of post-Egyptian, pre-ministry education in Wilderness U.? Even the mighty apostle Paul processed privately for fourteen years before God gave him a public platform. Based on Paul's candid admission of ongoing personal and spiritual struggles, his process was cast clearly in the lifelong mind-renewal mold. No wonder God used Paul to write about the need for us to keep on being transformed by the continual renewing of our minds. (That's a literal rendering of the Greek verb tenses in Romans 12:2.)

Perhaps part of our resistance to this change-is-the-journey rather than change-is-the-destination mindset relates to the unappealing prospect of ongoing emotional upheaval.

(Almost) Terror as a Price of Change

I chuckled to myself as I typed the heading to this section because I am imagining two possible responses. Some of you may be thinking, "Terror? There's no terror in changing." Others might be saying to themselves, "Almost? There's no *almost* to the terror of changing." I'm guessing that the first response characterizes change-rookies, while the second belongs to battle-scarred change-veterans.

Changing is very scary. If you haven't discovered that, I suspect you haven't been changing very much. I often use a circus analogy to picture the almost-terror level of fear I hear counselees describe when they are struggling with change.

Have you ever watched a trapeze act performing high above a circus floor? If so, you've seen a man or woman standing on a tiny platform or hanging from a trapeze bar as someone across the way swings a bar toward him or her. Now put yourself in the place of that man or woman. You see the trapeze bar coming; you reach out for it. But—to your horror—you discover you can't quite grasp it without first letting go of what you're already gripping or leaving the safety of your present perch. You're not sure you can afford to glance down to check the safety net—even if there is or ever was one!

I think we spend much of our changing, recovering, mending, healing journey in that midair split-second of terror between relinquishing the wounding, binding familiar places and firmly grasping the healing, freeing unfamiliar. At the beginning of our journeys, we probably hang there *most* of the time. (Sorry, but I'm committed to telling the truth!)

That breath-snatching, midair stretch of trembly transition is a mess-up and muddle-through place where endings alone beckon beginnings. Only losses guarantee gains. Rock-sure Gibraltars dissolve to quicksand under our feet in an experience as essential as it is unnerving.

When we've grown up in families where chaos spelled impending pain and disaster or—at the very least—increased emotional neglect, we're allergic to anything that feels off-balance, unstructured, uncertain—in a word—*chaotic.* We probably don't even like spontaneity. With such personal histories, the perfectly normal confusion and chaos of changing feels not just distressing to us, but dangerous, destructive and—yes—terrifying.

Nevertheless all the tears and years of time, and even the terror of transition, are worth the joy of changing. But because making and consistently practicing new, more truthful choices is such a difficult, disorienting enterprise, we all need more than just a plan. We need power.

A Power Source for Change

We are not truth-seeking, truth-loving creatures by nature—at least not those of us this side of Eden. Deceit is the natural current of our lives. So we desperately need a power source, maybe even a motivation source, outside our natural selves to propel and guide us in the swimming-upstream process of changing by consistently choosing truth.

Did you hear about the farmer who bought a chain saw that was guaranteed to cut five big trees an hour? The day after his purchase, he returned it to the store with obvious frustration. "Five trees an hour? It barely cut five trees the whole day," the angry farmer exclaimed. Puzzled, the store owner took the saw outside, jerked its cord, and started the powerful engine. The saw's deafening roar startled the farmer so badly, he stumbled and fell trying to escape. Regaining his balance he gasped, "What's that noise?"

Cutting trees with an unstarted chain saw is no more foolish than trying to "do recovery" or "get well" with our own strength alone. One of my favorite Scriptures, Zechariah 4:6, captures this truth: " 'Not by might nor by power, but by My Spirit,' / Says the Lord of hosts" (NKJV). We need to understand and commit to change. We need a plan to guide the process. But without the power of God's Spirit energizing our understanding, commitment, and process, we will go through the motions of change without anything significant happening.

Hurt people need significant healing. Mere superficial healing won't do the job. Human helpers can supply a lot of the latter; only God can supply the former. That's because our hurting is rooted in an issue that goes far deeper than childhood experiences.

The Bible describes it in one three-letter word: *SIN*. That's not a popular word these days. Nevertheless, Scripture indicates repeatedly that all human beings are sin-stained. More accurately we are sin-*slain*—dead spiritually because of our sins. (See Eph. 2:1.) Christians believe that Jesus Christ had no sin of his own, yet chose to come to earth to die for our sins so that we could experience the eternal quality of life that exists only in a personal relationship with him.

We must let him pilot our lives before we can ask him to power our changing. He won't barge in and take over, but he enters hearts when invited. Of course we have to own our responsibilities in the injury-recovery, healing-from-hurts changing process. But, just as there is an unseen, inner energy at work in *physical* healing and change, God's unseen Spirit energizes our emotional/spiritual changing processes when we let him. As we do our parts, God does his "inside job" to create change of eternal significance.

Pause to Ponder and Pray

PONDER: Great, gaping wounds need a *Great* Physician!
You already feel dead? Then you need a proven death defeater! I am delighted to introduce you to the one and only death defying, greatest healer and life-changer of all time: *Jesus of Nazareth.* (Check out his track record in the first four books of the New Testament.)

The most eternally significant, life-changing choice you will ever make is asking Jesus Christ to supervise your life and your healing/changing process.

If you haven't done that, you can do it right now by sincerely praying something like the following. (Remember, God cares more about your desire to know Jesus personally than the specific words you say.)

PRAY: Dear Jesus, I want to know you personally as my Savior, my Friend, and Lord of my life. Please come into my life and forgive me of my sins. Thank you for paying the sin debt I could never pay. Thank you for the free gift of your love. Please direct and empower my changing process. You know how scary it is for me, so thanks for being my safety net, too. Amen.

Just Ahead

In the following chapters, we'll see how we can begin to get help for the healing process in several hurting areas of our lives. Each step in this new-choices-for-change adventure requires putting away childish choice-things and purposefully walking in truth.

Let's get started by examining our self-inflicted wounds, the old choices that created them, and the new, healthier choices that bring healing.

CHAPTER
Eight

Help for Healing
Self-inflicted Wounds

"'Achy-breaky heart?' Man, that's nothin'. I've got an achy-breaky *life!*"

John sure made a hit with his support group when he adapted the title of a chart-topping Country-Western song and used it to summarize his change-process distress. How about you? Got any "achy-breaky" stuff going on in your heart or life? Considering the rough-and-tumble ride we unsuspectingly sign on for at birth, I guess we shouldn't be surprised.

Some of us got saddled with far more bruising birth-families than others. And as if the wounds we've received from family and "friends" were not sufficiently painful, the truth is that we've also wounded ourselves. In medicine the word *iatrogenic* refers to physical injuries resulting from medical treatment. Similarly, most of our self-inflicted wounds come from our attempts to treat our old inner wounds and protect ourselves from more wounding.

In this chapter we'll examine self-inflicted wounds in areas of self-concept, legitimate needs, and authentic emotions. After our diagnoses, we'll apply our change plans to each of these hurting areas.

Self-inflicted Self-concept Wounds

"I'm worth it!" A gorgeous actress directs that declaration into the television camera while tossing her gloriously blonde hair coquettishly over one exquisite shoulder.

How about you? Are you worth it? Are you worth knowing, worth respecting, worth loving? What sort of relationship do you have with yourself? Yes, that's right, you have a relationship with yourself. We all have some kind, you know. Do you treat yourself like a friend or an enemy? At this precise moment in your life, are you more actively involved in your growing/stretching/healing process or engaged in self-inflicted re-victimization?

Many of us think we're not "worth it," whatever *it* might be. We treat ourselves accordingly by regularly and relentlessly rewounding ourselves with shame.

Shame Wounds

I described binding (as differentiated from biblical) shame as the soul-deep sense that I am disgustingly different from and worth *less* than others. This sense of shame grows from a two-pronged lie:

- Humans can be perfect.
- Humans must be perfect to qualify for living and loving, that is, to qualify for existence and relationships.

Children learn binding shame if their earliest relationships are characterized by unrealistic expectations and/or neglect or abuse. If we hear "You ought to be ashamed" often enough and long enough, we believe it.

Eventually the shaming messages set up housekeeping inside our brains like tiny videotapes of shaming sounds and scenes. Our shame tapes play automatically every time we betray human imperfection and limitations by having problems, making mistakes, failing at tasks. Binding shame profoundly hinders our changing/healing processes because it means more self-inflicted wounds.

Shame says, "I don't have any wounds, self-inflicted or otherwise. I certainly don't need to change. Everything in my life is just perfect. Thanks for asking, anyway." If there's a remnant of such sentiment lurking in a corner of your mind, you need to know the high price tag attached.

Recently researchers found that people with "hidden psychological distress" are making themselves increasingly and needlessly vulnerable to illness:

> If you're unable or unwilling to admit your deepest emotions, you are more apt to get both mild and killer diseases—from colds, flu, and allergies to heart disease and cancer. . . . Not talking about upsetting events creates additional stress. And the failure to talk causes the damage to continually resurface.[1]

This research reflects the truth of Scripture, namely that we are foolish when we traffic in deception, especially self-deception. (See Prov. 14:8 for just one of many verses addressing this important principle.)

We can't seek or receive help for problems we can't admit we have. Instead most of us exhausted, discouraged, shame-bound folks do what we do best. We practice what my friend Jeff VanVonderen calls the three steps of shame: "trying, trying harder, and trying my hardest."[2] We also lock ourselves into energy-sapping, life-crushing patterns of perfectionism. Shame and its companion, existence guilt, grease the skids for life-crushing perfectionism. And perfectionism is profoundly wounding.

As a recovering perfectionist I know how difficult it is to risk being real about weaknesses and failings. I relapse regularly in my recovery. Then I berate myself for not being perfectly recovered from my perfectionism! Why do reasonably intelligent, sane adults start thinking and living like this? Again, early experiences and choices provide a context for understanding and changing.

Who I am is all I have of me. If who I am—just me, the *real* me—proves too unreliable to secure a safe place in the world and a nurturing level of acceptance and affection, I am disarmed. Since I have no other "being" resources with which to fight for your approval, I decide to switch instead from *being* to *doing*. I shift to a performance basis for my life that permeates every relational arena—with myself, God, and with others—since this is the arena where I first lost the permission to be who I am. Performance based self-concepts and lives get pretty painful and frantic since the more and better I do usually feels like the more and better I am.

We don't have to be rocket scientists to notice that, when we live this performance based lifestyle, in effect we give other people the power to determine our feelings of personal safety and worth. We become approval addicts who will do nearly anything for a fix. We jump through behavioral hoops

"IT'S AMAZING HOW WE FOUND EACH OTHER."

and twist ourselves into emotional pretzels to earn the approval of important people in our lives. And a whole lot of our hoop-jumping and pretzel-twisting deeply wounds us.

For instance, usually we learn pretty early in life that we earn a lot of approval by being helpful. So some of us become *helpaholics.* We develop an invisible radar system that ferrets out folks who need help, as the previous cartoon shows. But in our helping frenzies, we may neglect our own spouses and children, even our own health. Some of us are practically *dying* to help others. But, hey, that's what we're here for, right? Besides, they have so many needs while we don't have any.

Self-inflicted Wounds from Denying Authentic Needs

Out of our awareness, many of us decided in childhood that the best way to meet our needs was to eliminate them. The problem, of course, was that denying needs didn't make them disappear. In fact, ignoring our natural, human needs is a little like trying to hold your breath underwater. We ignore our lungs' cries for oxygen as long as possible—sometimes longer, it seems. The worst part is that for many of us, this is an enormous source of pride. In effect, the worse we feel, the better we feel! Many of us secretly glory in the fact that, while less hearty souls drop at our sides, we are able to work longer hours, sleep less, grab faster-food on the run to our next important meeting or people-helping commitment. Our sheer survival in the face of such killer schedules bolsters our shame-battered self-concepts.

The more shame-bound we are, the more intensely we need to push ourselves to multiply our daily allotment of minutes and maximize our productivity and helpfulness. Maybe if we work, rush, push, help, and really keep trying hard enough, we'll be almost barely good enough to earn our bosses', our friends', our pastors', and God's approval. And if we can just push a little harder, we may even earn our parents' approval too—someday. If our bodies hold up that long, that is.

Scripture declares that our bodies are "temple[s] of the Holy Spirit" that have been bought with a price by God, who created them (see 1 Cor. 6:19). And Psalm 139:14 says, "I praise you because I am fearfully and wonderfully made; / your works are wonderful, / I know that full well" (NIV). Indeed, God made our wonderful bodies, but it looks like a whole lot of us don't necessarily know that "full well." Consider the evidence.

Many of us wage war on our own bodies. Our weapons are sleep deprivation, zero or abusive exercise, chronic dieting, sleeping pills, fasting, overeating, bingeing and purging, relaxation deprivation, and many others. We engage in this temple demolition project for many different reasons, including mindlessly emulating the self-wounding, body-bashing lifestyles our parents modeled.

Some of us hate our bodies for betraying us by developing shapes that abusers blamed for their actions. Others of us despise our bodies for revealing pain by bleeding or for revealing sexual pleasure by experiencing orgasm. The latter is one of the most difficult, confusing, and humiliating realities sexual abuse survivors face. It is especially hard when the abuse perpetrator uses a victim's sexual response against her or him with statements like, "See, you really wanted me to do this because it makes you feel good."

I counseled with one incest survivor who felt genuine pride because she had learned to totally numb out any sexual responsiveness when she was abused as a child. That was her way of controlling some aspect of her out-of-control childhood, she said. Needless to say, she and her husband now experience the reality of her childhood solution becoming her adult life problem in the area of sexual responsiveness. This situation also illustrates how we wound ourselves in our self-protective efforts to prevent wounds.

Unless we've been living in caves lately, we've all heard or read about the accumulating mass of research demonstrating that our bodies and our emotions are inextricably bound together in a miraculous merger designed by God. This means that we wound our bodies when we wound our emotions.

Self-inflicted Wounds from Denying Emotions

Some of us have developed the skill of taking everything without feeling anything and have turned it into a badge of honor. Each of our stories is unique, of course, but there seems to be some gender-based differences in who is allowed to feel what.

" 'Big boys don't cry.' That's what I remember being told," Carl said as he described his frozen feelings. A successful professional and an active church member, Carl joined a Christ-centered support group because his marriage and personal life were in trouble. As the group discussed acceptable and unacceptable emotions in their childhood families, Carl began to see some of the roots of his present emotional paralysis.

"Big boys aren't ever afraid, either," Jerry said.

"And big boys don't admit they have problems by joining support groups, either." (This was my contribution at that point in the discussion. You see, Carl and Jerry were the only men in the nine person group. This men-to-women proportion is fairly typical. I mean, ask yourself, do you think John Wayne or Clint Eastwood would join a support group? Of course, women have their own variation of the unacceptable-emotions theme. For us, anger and confidence are usually off-limits.)

Wilson's Law of Emotions seems applicable at this juncture, namely: *Feelings are a fact and feelings have a history.* This means that both men and women feel sadness, fear, anger, and many other emotions. However, regardless of the emotions men and women can feel, both boys and girls learn very early which emotions are gender-acceptable in their families. They begin to filter all other feelings out of their awareness. In unhealthy families *unacceptable* is a code word for *dangerous,* because when we do the unacceptable in such families, we experience emotional and even physical pain as a result. So dangerous, unacceptable feelings must be denied and disowned. And the sooner the better.

I think children learn to dispose of unacceptable emotions by dumping them into their respective gender's Acceptable

Emotion Bin. This emotion dumping is a kind of recycling system that allows authentic emotions coming in at the top to be recycled into the most gender-acceptable feelings as the emotion crosses the person's awareness threshold. The diagram below depicts this self-protective, approval-securing emotion dumping and recycling process.

A Comparison of Male and Female "Emotion Recycling"

Male Emotion Recycling System	Female Emotion Recycling System
Sadness, Fear, and All Other "Soft" Emotions	Anger, Confidence, and All Other "Firm" Emotions

Awareness Threshold

ANGER BIN (a.k.a., "frustration")	DEPRESSION BIN (a.k.a., "concern")

Please note that most of us committed Christians are far too spiritual to ever be angry or depressed. So the evangelicalized bins are also known as "frustration" and "concern" for males and females respectively.

Anger warrants a special word since many people find intense anger and real rage far too frightening emotions to consider expressing them. The next cartoon captures our hearts' desires regarding rage, doesn't it? Remember, feelings like rage have a history. They are there to tell us that something in our lives hurts and needs tending.

Christians need to be reminded that anger is not a sin. (See Eph. 4:26.) It certainly isn't a sin to be angry at what angers God! God is very angry about all forms of child abuse. So why shouldn't we be? And why should we be any less angry about child abuse when the child is you or me? Jesus said the truth will make us free. The truth will make us mad, too, when part of the truth concerns wounding children.

Since feelings are a fact, denying, disowning, recycling, and relabeling them is not the same as destroying them. Whether we are supposed to feel the soft or the firm emotions, research indicates we wound ourselves when we refuse to recognize and respect chunks of our God-given emotional natures.

"HE'S HERE TO HAVE HIS RAGE REMOVED."

All this research highlights ways we wound ourselves by denying our feelings. We also wound ourselves when we try to deaden emotions with addictions.

Wounds from Addictions

When we deny the pain of unseen wounds, so we won't have to face our inner injuries, we inevitably wound ourselves. (Denial of reality always has that effect.) It's as if we end up crippling ourselves with our crutches.

I think that all addictions, whether legal or illegal, serve as emotional anesthetics. We use our addictions in an attempt to self-medicate the pain of living, especially the pain we think we shouldn't have. I've heard scores of counselees say, "I don't know what's wrong with me; I shouldn't feel like this." No matter what their "like this" was, those dear folks all had one thing in common. They didn't reckon on the second half of Wilson's Law of Emotions, because not only is a feeling a fact, every feeling has a history. Feelings don't just appear out of nowhere. Even if a feeling's history is primarily biochemical, it is extremely helpful to have that accurate context.

If we grew up in unhealthy families, we often face a double-bind situation with emotions. Those households typically elicit strong emotions much more often than less chaotic homes do. At the same time, hurtful families typically forbid most feelings. Consequently, children lack both the permission to feel their authentic emotions and the skills with which to express them appropriately.

If we were raised in these emotion-denying homes, we came into adolescence and adulthood desperate for substances or activities that would deaden our disallowed and disowned feelings, the feelings we "shouldn't" have, but do.

My drug of choice is chocolate. Affixed to the side of my refrigerator is a small poster obviously written by another chocoholic. It says: "Reality is an illusion produced by a chocolate deficiency."

Chocolate is an example of an *internal* addiction, which is an addiction to a substance that can be put into our bodies. The list of other internal addictions is endless. So is the list of external addictions—all those activities, events, and behaviors that can take over our lives, such as gambling, working, watching soap operas, and viewing pornography. What do all of these substances or activities have in common? They all have the ability to produce a pleasurable mood change, and that is the purpose of all addictions. However, all addictions, whether booze, bon-bons, or bargains, have several built-in problems.

First, all addictions have the same annoying side effect: they wear off. Second, all addictions get greedy. They start demanding bigger and bigger chunks of our lives—our thoughts, time, money, energy, integrity, reputation. (Technically, this side effect is called tolerance.) Eventually far too much of them becomes far too little to give us the positive emotional lift we want.

Third, all addictions ultimately add pain to our lives instead of subtracting it as we had hoped, or had been promised, because they all wound us to some degree. It is as if the ladder we thought we could use to escape a pit of pain turned out to be a shovel that just digs a deeper pit.

The truth behind these three points is this: When we use substances or activities to eliminate all our pain, we are on a fool's errand of insisting on the impossible. Mark it down, friend. Life brings pain, unavoidable pain. And the more we refuse to face our feelings and the unavoidable pain of our own unique histories, the more apt we are to keep searching for increasingly powerful mood altering fixes.

Christians, by the way, have their own denominationally approved addictions. For example, gambling is certainly off-limits (unless it's Bingo and you're a Catholic), while compulsive shopping and overspending rarely get mentioned. I can't imagine a congregation that wouldn't gasp in horrified disapproval if a drunk staggered down the aisle next Sunday. Yet week after week, life-threateningly obese or anorexic men and women all but stagger down the aisles of churches without notice. Some even stand behind pulpits. And the somewhat sanctified workaholism and evangelical hyperactivity that masquerade as deep religious commitment usually earn conspicuous congratulations, rather than compassionate confrontations in most churches.

Clearly, we can wound ourselves in a zillion ways. What began as a self-defensive protection usually becomes a self-defeating problem. How can we change such a pattern?

Applying the Change Plan to Self-inflicted Wounds

As we turn this corner to focus on changing our self-wounding ways, I have two caveats. The first is a reminder; the second is a warning.

You'll recall that my change formula is very simple:

NEW CHOICES + CONSISTENT PRACTICE = CHANGE

You may recall, too, that many of us unknowingly chose, and continue to choose to live as if we don't have choices. This keeps us functioning, in part, as children. When we continue to feel childified, we turn our backs on the priceless privilege of personal choice and slam the door on hope for change. So let's begin our change emphasis with a recommitment to reclaiming our choices.

Now for the warning.

You know those diamond-shaped roadside signs that warn us to proceed with caution because of what's just ahead? Well, instead of a warning to proceed with care, I'm erecting a warning sign reading:

PROCEED
WITH PRAYER—
MORE PAIN IS JUST
AROUND THE
CORNER

I think we need this extra caution sign because it can be terrifyingly painful when we actually begin practicing some of the following suggestions while laying aside our self-wounding, lifelong self-defenses. We made our earliest choices about how to keep ourselves safe and acceptable so long ago, we probably can't remember living any other way. We may feel as if we and our defenses are one.

These self-protective patterns are not just woven into the fabric of our lives. They seem to be grafted onto the tissues of our beings; we cannot painlessly put them away as childish things without inward tearing and even some emotional hemorrhaging. Know this, and believe this. It is true. Still, we *must* put these patterns away, because they are rooted in lies. And we are called to truth.

Healing Self-concept and Perfectionism Wounds

Here are some helpful, practical suggestions for change in these areas of your life.

1. *Settle in your heart and mind the difference between self-focus and self-awareness*. While an intense, temporary self-focus is almost always necessary to launch a purposeful changing process, the goal is a wise, realistic self-awareness. People who lack self-awareness are both unnecessarily vulnerable and quite dangerous.

2. *Begin learning who you really are*. God has an unmarred mirror into which we can look to see our true identities,

according to James 1:23. It's the Bible, of course. Use the verses listed in Appendix B to get you started on your true identity quest.

3.   *Redefine yourself and key people in your life from a more mature and truthful perspective.* As you review your childhood realities, you need to redefine them, too, because one of the primary characteristics of any abusive system is perpetrator-defined reality. So, "I am a slut and that's why my loving daddy had intercourse with me from the time I was age three until I was nine," becomes, "I am an incest survivor because my father repeatedly raped me when I was a child."

As your healing progresses, you will probably redefine yourself more than once as any childhood abuse or other hurts remain significant parts of your personal history without claiming the core of your identity.

Healing Self-inflicted Needs-Denial Wounds

If you spent your early years in a hurting, hurtful family where little or no emotional nurturing was available, you survived the pain of that by learning to deaden and deny your needs. Sadly many who made that early childhood choice still think there's no alternative.

These are some specific truth honoring ways to begin respecting your legitimate needs.

1.   *Learn to identify your long-denied needs.* Many of you have survived by concentrating on giving the important people in your lives what they wanted so completely that you neglected to develop the skill of listening to your own needs. This issue arose in one of the incest survivors' groups I led not long ago. Darla, a bright, sensitive Christian, identified the problem this way: " 'Well, she looks pretty healthy to me.' That's what Mark's (Darla's husband) brother said when Mark told him how painful my counseling is right now."

As Darla and the other incest survivors talked, they realized they had all refined the skill of hiding their genuine neediness and pain to help them survive as

children.   Their automatic I'll-look-fine-no-matter-
what stances, which are actually symptoms of their
wounds, had been masking their wounds so successfully that most people never knew they needed help.
Naturally no one offered any help.   What a classic
example of being crippled by our crutches!

2.   *Begin to see your body as clean from all past abuse*
whether you were the victim or the victimizer, or both. 1
John 1:7 says that "the blood of Jesus Christ [God's] Son
cleanses us from all sin." I've long known this verse is
extraordinarily encouraging; it certainly has been to me.
In my previous three books I've emphasized this verse
specifically by noting that *all* either really means *every*
sin or God is lying. God did not include *all* just to make
the print come out even on that page of the Bible!
As I've continued to meditate on God's outrageously
inclusive *all*, the implication has expanded even more.
Usually when we think of our sins, we think only of
the sins we have committed.   Right?   If *all* means
every possible kind of sin, then it is more than just our
sins against others.   *All* includes others' sins against
us.   In many cases, someone else sinned against our
bodies for years.   And some of us have used our bodies
to sin against others.   In effect our bodies may have
been the containers of sin as well as the conveyers of
sin.   So it's just like our awesomely thorough God to
include our bodies in the complete cleansing of his
dear children.
If you are an incest, satanic ritual abuse, or rape
survivor and/or perpetrator, you especially need to
memorize and meditate upon the personal im-
plications of Hebrews 10:22:

> Let us draw near to God with a sincere heart in full
> assurance of faith, having our hearts sprinkled to
> cleanse us from a guilty conscience and having our
> bodies washed with pure water. (NIV)

Please reread that verse. Do you realize what it means? It means that my body has been cleansed from my stepuncle's dirty, degrading sexual abuse. It means the same for each of you whatever your own body's sin history.

We must remember that the consequences of years of sins against our bodies do not disappear just because we sincerely give our hearts and lives to Jesus. Nevertheless in God's sight we are clean—spirits, souls, and bodies. (See 1 Thess. 5:23.)

3.   *Begin treating your body respectfully.* This includes the obvious, such as healthful sleep, exercise, and nutrition. Purposefully seek creative and genuinely enjoyable ways to do this, especially the exercise part. And don't forget to relax. If you're like me, you probably have a history of relaxation deprivation. If you clear the I-have-a-right-to-relax hurdle, you might consider a real stretch—playing. (Even though play is a four-letter word, it isn't obscene.)

4.   *Schedule time for you.* I know this means making some changes in your routine. That's the point. Freeing a slice of time for you sends a clear message to you and others that you respect yourself and your healing process. I frequently let my answering machine take calls when I am home and want uninterrupted time. Before I owned an answering machine, I simply took the phone off the hook.

If you have preschool children at home or you work long hours, finding time for you is more challenging, to be sure. But don't give up. Try swapping child care with a friend who also wants some just-for-me time. If you work outside the home, use your lunch hour more creatively. Several days a week, find a restful place to be alone with your thoughts and feelings. You could read Scripture and pray, close your eyes and daydream, or write in your journal.

Healing Self-inflicted Emotional Wounds

Continuing our old patterns of living, as if not feeling or showing our emotions is the same as not having them, is choosing to keep living a lie. What's more, it's a guaranteed, fail-safe way to never experience significant healing. For those of us who are tired of that hurtful way, the following ideas can get us turned toward change.

1. Use Appendix C to assess your beliefs about emotions. Think how different your life would be if you consistently practiced living based on the more shame-free, truthful beliefs. Discuss your thoughts with your friends, group, or counselor. Most importantly, begin putting feet to these truthful beliefs with new choices.

2. Find a safe place to feel and appropriately express your authentic emotions. This is what individual and group counseling ideally provide. Truly healthy Bible study groups may do the same, depending on the intensity of your emotional wounds.

3. Please seek help immediately to get free of such heavy-duty addictions as alcohol, cocaine, other illegal drugs, and prescription tranquilizers. Don't try to follow a Lone Ranger Recovery Program. Admitting the problem to others and asking for help is an indispensable part of your healing.

Healing for Self-inflicted Wounds: H.O.P.E.

We've established the necessity of keeping a process perspective in our changing/healing work. Yet while we tighten our seat belts for the lifelong journey, it helps to have some markers to indicate our progress. So here, and near the end of most of the following chapters, I'll include a Healing Overview and Progress Evaluation (H.O.P.E.) chart. It will list the major issues covered in the chapter, along with very brief descriptions of three significant stages of any recovering work, whether from seen or unseen injuries.

Self-inflicted Wounds Healing Overview and Progress Evaluation (H.O.P.E.) Chart

KEY ISSUES	SEEING TRUTH	NEW CHOICES	NEW PRACTICING
Performance based worth	See what I've been *doing* to earn the right to *be*	Letting myself learn who I *really* am as God sees me	Learning to treat myself with the respect due all of God's children
Perfectionism	Believing the Bible that *all* people are flawed	Giving myself the right to be wrong	Learning to accept my flaws without indulging them
Denying my own needs	Realizing I have real human needs	Starting to identify my real human needs	Learning to get my needs met appropriately
Denying my real feelings	Recognizing I have more emotions than those in my "bin"	Giving myself permission to identify real feelings	Learning to express authentic emotions appropriately

---

Pause to Ponder and Pray

PONDER: Use the H.O.P.E. chart to get an idea of where you are in your changing and healing process. Please remember this isn't a contest! So consistently practice *not* comparing yourself and your progress to someone else and theirs. That's tough to avoid if we were motivated in childhood with unfavorable comparisons. Read 2 Corinthians 10:12 to get God's view of such motivation.

PRAY: Lord, please help me believe you when you tell me who I am as a child in your family. Thank you, Jesus, for being perfect, because I've tried so hard for so long and have never been able to be. Amen.

Just Ahead

We've already discovered that all of the issues covered in separate chapters overlap and interact. For example, when we are on a performance-based treadmill, unable to distinguish between commitment to excellence and pathological perfectionism, we not only wound ourselves, we structure all our relationships in ways that inevitably wound others, too. Let's take a closer look at this in the next few chapters.

CHAPTER
Nine

Help for Healing
Friends and Spouses

Do you know what the problem is with my friends? They're all a bunch of sinners! Seriously—every last one. That's why I fit right in with them.

Human relationships are endless cycles of inflicting and enduring, tending and grieving inner wounds. Because Sinners-R-Us, this cycle likely will not come to a screeching halt without divine intervention. (To which, by the way, I personally look forward.) In the meantime, reducing the size, depth, and frequency of interpersonal wounding is a more reasonable and achievable goal. That's what we'll talk about in this chapter.

New Wounds from Old Patterns

We'll discover quickly how the issues covered in separate chapters overlap and interact. If we're perfectionists, for example, we fear making mistakes or failing in any area of life. Yet both are inevitable. If our mistakes or failures draw criticism, our performance-based self-concepts take a tumble. Since we can't tolerate criticism from others in any form, we react defensively and alienate those close to us. This only reinforces our beliefs that we must be perfect to be accepted. What a mess!

Again, we face the truth that what we learned in our birth families shaped every area of our lives as the cartoon clearly depicts. This is why it's been said that all adult relationships are, to some degree, family reunions.

"I WONDER WHAT SHE SEES IN HIM?"

The big news from the 1992 conference of the American Psychological Association was a study validating the idea that unexamined childhood perceptions create a kind of sitting-duck syndrome. Research with over seven hundred university women demonstrated that those who "experienced rape or attempted rapes as adolescents had a 239 percent greater chance than other women of experiencing rape or attempted rape during the first year in college." The study also found that women who had experienced family violence or sexual victimization before age fourteen had a 244 percent greater chance of encountering adolescent rape or attempted rape than other women.

It's astounding that my mental health colleagues and the Associated Press were so impressed by the thought that childhood victimization sets people up for repeated victimization in adult life. To use my husband's expression, that's a no-brainer! It is merely twentieth century evidence for first century truth that children can be caused to stumble into thinking and relating patterns that have long-term, devastating results.

The study's director noted that "childhood experiences may affect a child's sense of what healthy relationships are like and encourage behaviors that may make them more vulnerable to later assault."[1]

May? Where else would we learn about relationships except through our childhood experiences? Because our earliest relationships occurred within our families, we simply assumed that the way our family relationships were was the way *all* relationships were and were supposed to be.

I believe that when substantially healthy parents model biblical patterns of relating, they inoculate their daughters and sons against abusive adult relationships. Unfortunately boys and girls growing up in hurting and hurtful homes usually miss learning the basics about healthy relationships.

The Basics of Healthy Relationships

When I say in conferences that "many of us wouldn't know a healthy relationship if it bit us on the nose," people always chuckle. I've noticed that they also nod vigorously in recognition of an uncomfortable truth for most adults raised in hurtful families. Through the trial and error of tears and years, some of us have learned how to have reasonably healthy relationships. Others of us are still pretty befuddled by the whole thing. So let's begin our examination of relationships with a brief look at the two foundational pillars of healthy relating.

Mutual Respect and Responsibility

When two individuals have respect for themselves and for others, they have one-half the foundation for healthy relationships. In mutually respectful relationships, we uphold one another's right to separate opinions and choices. We can do this because we respect our own opinions and choices enough that we don't need to have them constantly validated by blatantly or subtly manipulating others into agreeing with us.

In interpersonal relationships, as in all other areas of our lives, we must operate from truth. This means that we respect others because they bear God's image and are the objects of his love. And we complete this truth by remembering that the image is marred by a sin nature, and others may reject God's love.[2] Therefore, it's unrealistic, unbiblical, and dangerously naive to expect every person we know to be honest and trustworthy.

When we balance an emphasis on mutual respect with a realistic understanding of human nature, we won't expect to always admire or even tolerate everything others do. With this balanced and truthful perspective in mind, we will relate with realistic respect toward ourselves and toward others.

Respecting others as much as we respect ourselves means letting other adults be as responsible for the consequences of their choices as we are for ours. Mutual responsibility provides the second foundational pillar for healthy relating.

When mutual respect and responsibility characterize our relationships, we will be safe, but we won't be hurt-free. Because we and those with whom we interact are human, we will unintentionally wound one another. But this is vastly different from what occurs in unhealthy relating.

As we shift our focus to unhealthy relationships, we will see that they express the self-protective choices we made in response to the three basic must-answer questions we faced as youngsters.

Relational Defenses for Answering the Question of Safety

You may recall that perhaps the most basic of all questions is: "Can I be safe?" When we feel safe in a secure family environment, we can allow people into our lives, based on our personal preferences. But when we choose to trust only ourselves to stay safe, we usually operate from one of two extremes related to interpersonal distance and closeness.

Those of us I call "Porcupines" keep ourselves safe by keeping others at a distance—all others. At a great distance. In stark contrast, some of us are more like an Octopus. Faster than a speeding bullet, we enfold, wrap around, enmesh, cling to, entangle, and entwine our relational tentacles with anyone in our paths—leaping tall boundaries of personhood in a single bound. Said differently, we have that intense urge to merge!

These relating extremes address issues of personal boundaries—the sense of where we end and where others begin. Healthy personal boundaries are neither too open and permeable, allowing everything and everyone in, nor too closed and impermeable, creating walls that keep everything and everyone out. The chart below contrasts healthy boundaries with the Octopus and Porcupine extremes.

Comparing Healthy and Unhealthy Personal Boundaries[3]

TOO PERMEABLE (Octopus Style)	APPROPRIATELY PERMEABLE (Healthy Style)	IMPERMEABLE (Porcupine Style)
I talk at an intimate level at the first meeting. I instantly, totally trust everyone I meet.	I don't overwhelm people with personal information. I allow time for trust to develop.	I don't ever open up, even to people I know to be trustworthy and caring.
I am overwhelmed and preoccupied with a person and his/her needs.	I am able to keep relationships in perspective and function effectively in other areas of my life.	I don't let myself even think about another person I'm interested in.
I can fall in love with a new acquaintance.	I know love is based on respect and trust; these take time to develop.	I don't ever let loving feelings develop with anyone.

TOO PERMEABLE (Octopus Style)	APPROPRIATELY PERMEABLE (Healthy Style)	IMPERMEABLE (Porcupine Style)
I let others determine my reality.	I believe my perceptions are as accurate as anyone's.	I am unwilling to listen to others' perceptions.
I let others direct my life.	I make decisions for myself based on God's leading of my choices.	I refuse to consider the opinions of others.
I don't ever notice when others invade my personal boundaries.	I notice when others try to make decisions for me, are overly helpful, and/or don't consult me about planning my time.	I never allow anyone to help me or give me ideas and suggestions even when it is helpful and appropriate.
I sacrifice my values if necessary to feel close to significant others.	I am not willing to do anything to maintain a relationship. I have biblical values that are not negotiable.	I am never willing to change anything I do to please anybody.

Understanding the Porcupine and Octopus Trusting Extremes

How does over-closeness or over-distancing make us feel safe? The latter relating extreme seems the more obvious answer, I suppose. To use combat imagery, I could stay safe by not letting you within range. That's a clue to the rationale behind under-trusting and over-distancing. Early in life over-distancers learned that when people get within firing range, so to speak, they fire. That means wounds. And having been wounded, we're apt to self-protectively steer clear of close relationships in the future. Daren is the quint-essential Porcupine who doesn't trust anyone. His chaotic and abusive childhood convinced him that trusting and being open anytime with anyone always brings pain. So as an adult, Daren uses under-trusting as a kind of magic shield to protect himself from more relational wounding and pain.

The Octopus defense seems less logical at first glance. However, I think I've unraveled the illusive logic behind this super-glue relating style. We touchy-feely, boundary-invad-ing over-trusters seem to believe that if, in a gush of instan-taneous total trusting, we spill our innermost longings and intimate vulnerabilities to virtual strangers, we will magi-cally transform even the lowest low-life into a paragon of trustworthy virtue.

"Surely, they won't hurt or abandon me when they know how much I'm trusting them," we seem to say. But they often do, because all the trusting in the world cannot create a trustworthy person without that person's cooperation, as Anne learned to her sorrow.

Anne, a bright and beautiful incest survivor, sobbed convulsively as she told me about her sexual relationship with a co-worker. "I just knew the minute I met him that I could trust him completely," she said about the older man who fathered her child. (This is a classic Octopus statement.) This "wise and kind man," as Anne described him, said he loved her and promised they would marry as soon as he settled some "minor personal problems."

Anne never asked her lover any details about his life or problems, because she didn't want him to think she didn't trust him. You can guess this man's response when Anne told him that she was pregnant and would like to get married immediately. This "wise and kind" lover laughed and told her that he already had a wife and family he had no intention of leaving. His parting comment to Anne was: "You're too naive for your own good." Unfortunately that trust bandit was right.

Appropriate Trusting, Relational Safety, and Intimacy

Although we don't usually recognize it, trusting is always a choice. When we trust appropriately we make reasonable choices based on other people's records of consistent (not perfect) reliability. But instead of learning to trust appropriately, extreme under- or over-trusters, like Daren and Anne, keep trusting in their magical self-protective relational styles to keep them safe from more wounds and pain. Isn't it amazing how resilient that childhood I-can-cause-events-and-control-people fantasy is? It seems to have more lives than a hundred cats!

When we Darens and Annes insist on relating by magical childhood fantasies, inevitably we feel more isolated and abandoned. This confirms our shame-shaped different-and-worthless self-concepts, and keeps us believing the lie that our imperfection disqualifies us from loving relationships. We won't risk removing our masks of perfection or moving out of trusting extremes. Those self-protective choices directly relate to the question: "Can I be me?" And our answers to that identity question directly impact our answers to: "Can I be accepted?"

Relational Defenses Answering Identity and Attachment Questions

Can I be me? As many of us from hurtful families concluded, not really. Each of us has strengths and weaknesses. But if I'm shame-bound and believe I must earn the right to exist and be in a relationship, I might center my identity on always being strong and never showing weakness, so I can take care of others.

Here's the logic behind such a self-protective choice. If I am deeply shame-wounded, I can't comprehend that any reasonably healthy person would freely choose to relate to me. But if you are really weak and terribly needy, you might be desperate enough to keep me in your life to take care of you. In effect, we have to make ourselves indispensable precisely because we believe we're so worthless.

The more we believed, as children, that we would never earn the right to be close to people or be affirmed for our achievements if anyone suspected we weren't flawless and problem-proof, the more we are apt to spend our adult lives in unbalanced, disrespectful, or even abusive relationships. We might join the ranks of the rescuers who go behind the people we're saving and sort of mop up the personal messes they leave. I mean we clean up all the financial, legal, and other kinds of predicaments they create, so they don't have to cope with all the untidy results of their own inappropriate behavior.

When we take this so-called strong position in a relationship, we are saying that the answer to "Can I be accepted?" is: "Only as the need-*ee*, can I feel snugly and securely attached to a need-*er*."

Some of us who play strong rescuer roles endure degrading and even dangerous situations in the name of love. Ironically, we always wind up feeling controlled when we attempt to control others. (We do that only for their own good, of course.) I will be able to appropriately and lovingly detach from you unless I am trying to control your behavior and/or especially your opinion of me. If I'm determined to control either, you can tell me (directly or indirectly) to stand on my head while stacking greased BBs and I'll do it. My desire to control you allows you to control me.

The truth is that unless I am in prison or in a hostage-taking or some other situation involving physical duress, I—as an unimpaired adult—cannot be your victim. That makes me a volunteer, not a victim. I probably won't recognize that I'm volunteering, but that doesn't change the fact that I am. This is a great example of why we must come to the place of recognizing our self-defensive choices. If I don't know I have chosen to play victim in certain relationships, I won't realize I can choose a healthier relational style.

In contrast, some adults choose a defensive interpersonal style that springs from their identities as weak, under-responsible, helpless victims. From this perspective, we seem to feel relationally safer being the need-*ers*. We stay helpless enough to virtually force any reasonably decent person into helping us. We give up trying to earn anything, and settle instead for taking as a way to feel safe and stay connected to all the rescuers who live to give. In effect, we play a victim role in life.

We must clearly understand that children do not play a victim role or freely choose such a relational position in their birth families. *Neglected and abused children are victims*! Sadly, some genuinely victimized children unknowingly choose to remain in the victim role, even when they get older and other options are available.

The following chart summarizes the over-responsible, strong rescuer and under-responsible, weak victim styles of relating contrasted with the more balanced, healthy position.

Personal Responsibility Extremes[4]

WEAK VICTIM (Under-responsible)	HEALTHY ADULT (Responsible for Self)	STRONG RESCUER (Over-responsible)
I am so weak I am a wreck.	I have strengths and weaknesses. I am a human being.	I am so strong I am a rock.
I have no responsibility for anyone or anything.	I am responsible *for* myself *and to* others.	I am responsible for everything/everyone.
I can't change anybody.	I can change only myself.	I can change everybody.
I need someone to take care of me all the time.	I can take care of myself most of the time. I trust God to care for me at all times.	I will take care of you all the time.
Everything is too much for me.	Some things are too much for me, but nothing is ever too much for God.	Nothing is too much for me.
I desperately need you.	I desperately need God, and I long for relationships.	I desperately need to be needed.

Children in hurtful families often must play both victim and rescuer. Incest victims, for example, are typically forced to rescue their abusers from legal consequences by keeping the incest secret. If we come from hurtful families and we haven't done some healing and changing, we will likely continue to bounce between victim and rescuer roles in the same or different relationships. Rescuers must have, or must create, victims, and victims always need to find rescuers. Both roles are disrespectful and destructive to individuals, not to speak of relationships.

What happens if we attempt to move out of those two roles? As surely as night follows day, we get forced into a third.

The Karpman Triangle and the Wilson Rectangle

There are only three roles available in unhealthy, unbalanced, and unbiblical relationships: rescuer, persecutor, and victim. We move from one position to another when we're stuck in this tricornered relational trap.

It is what Melody Beattie calls "The Karpman Drama Triangle" in her bestseller, *Codependent No More*.[5] Picture a triangle with the words *rescuer, persecutor,* and *victim* at each corner. Here's the way it works: You ask if you can borrow my credit card because you've overloaded yours.

RESCUER CORNER: As long as I allow you to use my credit card, I will be keeping you from tasting the sour fruit of your spendthrift lifestyle. As long as I continue to occupy the rescuer corner of the Karpman Triangle, you will think I'm kind and generous.

VICTIM CORNER: As I continue to disrespect you by not expecting you to be as responsible for your debts as I am for mine, I might have to find a second job, cut back my spending, or whatever. Under my breath, I may mumble something like, "Why am I always the one getting hurt when all I wanted to do was help?" Of course I'll say it very softly so no one hears and concludes that I am unsympathetic or—worse yet—selfish, because I'm thinking about myself. Clearly, I've arrived at the victim corner.

PERSECUTOR CORNER: What if my usually empty credit card is approaching critical mass no matter how hard I work, and I finally tell you that your free ride is over? You may tell me (and others, probably) that I am unsympathetic and judgmental. There I sit, smack dab in the persecutor position. If my sense of personal identity, safety, and worth depends on being loved by everyone I meet, I may buckle under the painful pressure of the persecutor role. I may continue our unbalanced, unhealthy relationship by rescuing you again and moving back to the rescuer corner.

This same role-shifting occurs when we begin at the victim position. All people-helpers recognize the classic examples of child abuse survivors who decide to stop rescuing their abusers and to start telling the truth. Without fail, abuse-protecting families perceive these courageous truth-telling survivors as persecutors who are stirring up trouble.

Can you see that in unhealthy relationships we are doomed to ping-pong back and forth from the role of victim to rescuer? There's no way to end this deadly cycle except to endure the pain of being perceived as a persecutor for choosing truth and healing. That's because unhealthy relational systems do not include an option of balanced, biblical, mutual one-another-ing.

The New Testament uses the phrase "one another" several times to describe relationships marked by mutuality. Obviously, one-anothering relationships exhibit a healthy balance, because both people take responsibility for doing what Scripture exhorts. A healthy balance is not just you being kind and forgiving while I continue being cruel and hurtful.

As I've reflected on the personal and relational qualities necessary for these balanced, biblical interactions, I created this two-by-two cell I call "The Wilson Relationship Rectangle." It shows the interaction of personal responsibility and respect for others in four relational positions.

The Wilson Relationship Rectangle

		RESPECT FOR OTHERS	
		HIGH	LOW
RESPONSIBILITY FOR SELF	High	ONE-ANOTHERING "You're worth respecting and being responsible for yourself and so am I."	RESCUER "You're a mess and I'm a mop."
	Low	VOLUNTEER VICTIM "You're worth whatever I have to endure from you."	USER-ABUSER "You're a resource and I'm a user."

We've discussed the rescuer, volunteer victim, and biblical one-anothering positions, but the user-abuser role in unhealthy adult relationships needs some explanation. When hurting and hurtful folks are blatantly abusive (by battering with fists or words, for example), we can spot them easily or with minimal help. Sometimes though, their "you are a resource for me to use for my purpose and pleasure" attitude comes out differently. I heard about a bachelor farmer who advertised for a wife. His ad read: "Man 35, wants woman about 25, with tractor. Send picture of tractor." Some of us seek relationships with people who seek tractors! No wonder we keep feeling used.

As you can see, the Wilson Rectangle includes a healthy relational position encompassing both a high degree of personal responsibility and a high respect for others. Adopting such a relating style could alter our entire social lives!

Usually without knowing it, many of us spend our adult years scanning our environments to find people who resemble our folks or other important adults from our childhoods. Each of these adult-life stand-ins offers us a next time, as in, "Next time I'll be lovable enough to make him/her stay with me forever."

"WILL YOU MARRY ME...
AND BE MY MOM?"

The cartoon depicts a matrimonially minded young man who seems to understand himself quite well. Most of us don't see or acknowledge our relational repetition patterns so clearly.

Some peoples' ideas of a fifty/fifty relationship include: I dirty, you clean; I spend, you earn. In other words, I choose to be under-responsible, so you must choose to be over-responsible. Whichever responsibility style we choose, it creates problems, and these problems show up most clearly in that most intimate relationship, marriage.

The Special Challenges of Marriage

Most of us give more thought to purchasing a new car than to selecting a mate. The more shame-bound our self-concepts, the more we operate from a painful-love-is-better-than-no-love-at-all perspective. When we do, we unknowingly ignore clear signs of a potential spouse's hurtful ways, such as jealousy, verbal abuse, unrealistic expectations, hypersensitivity, and/or blaming others for problems. We won't even stop to ask ourselves simple, basic questions like:

- Am I willing to spend my life with this person if he or she never changed one bit from the way he or she is at this very moment?

- Would I want to become more like this person just as she or he is now?

- Would I want this person, just as he or she is now, to be the father or mother of my children?

- Would I want my children to be just like this person as she or he is right now?

These four questions obviously address one of the giant pitfalls to healthy marriages: Many of us don't commit to romantic partnerships so much as we contract for *renovation projects*. We undertake complete overhauls of our spouses before the wedding cake gets stale.

This approach to marriage expresses the shame-bound belief that "You must be perfect because your real role is to prove that I can attract a perfect person, and that will keep others from discovering that I'm imperfect." But healthy marriages are based not only on mutual realistic respect and balanced responsibility, but also on accepting a spouse "as is."

Nora, a growing, changing, thirty-something daughter of perfectionistic parents, found the "as is" approach was unfamiliar but freeing. She told her Christian support group, "When I first started facing my perfectionistic demands on myself, I began to see the impossible stuff I was expecting from my husband. He was always angry and I was always disappointed and depressed. Lately I've started thinking of

him like the seconds for sale in a linen outlet. I mean, it helps
to see him as good but imperfect merchandise that I agreed
to take 'as is.' After all, isn't that the way God agreed to take
me?"

Indeed it is. What's more, God repeatedly and clearly tells
us that. We could say that his agenda for interacting with us
is as up-front and open as we can humanly receive. But in
contrast, we often hide our agendas.

Hidden Agendas in Marriage

One reason our spouses greatly anger and disappoint us so
often is that we keep insisting they love us unconditionally.
They can't. They never will. Some come closer than others,
but no person can do the humanly impossible. No one can
totally rise above their own needs and desires in order to
totally meet ours.   Yet that's usually the deep desire and
hidden agenda many of us carry over the threshold as we
enter marriage. But, even as we do, most of the time we hide
these desires and agendas from ourselves, as well as our
spouses. All we know is we have deep, unidentified longings
in our lives, and we expect our unsuspecting spouses to
satisfy them. But they have their own longings and agendas.

Our vague feelings that something is missing in us fuel a
kind of fill-up fantasy. It is as if marriage is like a long stop
at a gas station where each empty-feeling spouse says to the
other, "Drain the pain and fill'er up with joy." With this
agenda, each spouse's sweetly murmured I do's can be translated, "I do promise to let you spend your every waking
moment kissing the painful boo-boo's of my life to take away
all my hurts and make me feel better. And if you do, I promise
to stay with you." This demand for personal fulfillment from
other empty people is as reasonable as seeking blood from
turnips or water from stones. We can't miss the sad irony of
this approach to relationships in general and marriage in
particular. Scripture uses the imagery of broken wells to
convey this point in Jeremiah 2:13.

While our individual agendas differ, one of the most common hidden agendas for spouses raised in hurtful families
centers on the emotion-laden issue of loyalty.

Hidden Agendas of Divided Loyalty

Many of us, as well as our spouses, have never transferred our primary loyalties from our birth-families to the families established when we married. We never learned that we should or could. This is the leaving-and-cleaving principle of Genesis 2:24. God tells spouses (husbands, specifically) to separate from their parents and inseparably bond to their mates. But we can't leave and cleave while simultaneously maintaining our full-fledged status as loyal children if our parents decide to punish us for leaving.

Bill came from a hurtful, mediocrity-exalting family that ridiculed him as a child for his expanding vocabulary. Family members made statements such as, "Well, listen to Mr. Bigshot here. He thinks his fancy words make him smarter than the rest of us, who talk in plain ol' English." Bill quickly learned to live down to his family's expectations to avoid the raucous laughter that typically followed such comments.

Neither of Bill's parents finished high school. Both seemed amazed that their son wanted to graduate and go on to the state university where he had a full athletic scholarship. Bill met his future wife, Alice, in college. This is how he describes his struggle with divided loyalties: "Alice's folks always encouraged their kids to express themselves to the best of their abilities. I envied Alice's great vocabulary, but, of course, I would never admit that. And I sure wasn't about to start increasing mine and risk my family's ridicule.

"When Alice used big words around our two sons to help them expand their verbal skills, I ridiculed her in front of them. Wanting to be 'real men' like their dad, they soon learned to belittle her, too, and articulate speech in general. To this day both boys have very limited vocabularies. I would give anything if only I had realized earlier what I was doing to my boys, and to my wife! Somehow I thought I was supposed to live by my parents' values forever, and I was too afraid of losing their approval if I didn't. But come to think of it, I never really felt like I had their approval anyway."

Bill and Alice eventually sought counseling to strengthen their wobbly marriage. Both worked hard at changing, and both learned that we must move commitment to our spouses ahead of commitment to our parents.

Marriage and Ways That Seem Right

Proverbs describes a way that seems right to us, but it is a way that ends in death (see Prov. 14:12). Some spouses, or spouse wanna-be's, attempt to guarantee marital success in various ways that seem right. During the 1960s and '70s, for example, the popular view said that living together before marriage increased a couple's chances for success. However, that was a myth. Researchers recently found that "cohabitating experiences significantly increase young people's acceptance of divorce."[6] We've also learned that there are other, equally ineffective ways of trying to guarantee marital happiness.

I know of spouses who allow their mates to assault their children, "to keep the family together." This travesty may seem right, but it is death to the concept of family as God designed it. Parents are responsible for protecting their children until they are adults, even when one spouse must protect the children from the other spouse. Sometimes an abuse-enabling spouse is actually most concerned about preserving the family's facade to keep the marriage from being labeled a failure.

Divorce is a failure. It produces unforeseen pain and trauma for everyone involved, especially the children. No wonder God says he hates divorce. And no wonder we lose hope about the prospects for healing our hurting, hurtful relationships. But we can change them, and here are a few ways to begin.

Specific Change Strategies

Remember, change principles apply only to changing *ourselves*, because I am the only person I can change. We need this reminder as we look at some specific ways to begin healing broad relational wounds.

Changing General Relational Wounds

1. *Read the New Testament specifically looking for relational principles.* Notice especially how Jesus related. Use Appendix D to get an idea of how to draw relational principles and personal applications from biblical passages. Write about your discoveries, thoughts, and feelings in your personal journal. Talk with a trusted friend or counselor about what you wrote.

2. *Practice appropriate trusting by using Share-Check-Share.* This strategy helps both under- and over-trusters. Share-Check-Share is the process of sharing a small part of ourselves and then stopping to check the other person's response. If he or she is respectful and interested, it probably is safe to share a bit more another time. If not, we won't feel totally rejected since we shared only a small part of us.[7]

Changing Marital Relational Wounds

1. *Apply the general principles of healthy, biblical relating in your marriage.* It's surprising that we often relate and communicate using healthy principles in the workplace or elsewhere, but neglect to take them home with us.

2. *Read books, attend seminars, and talk to genuinely healthy married couples to learn how you can be a less hurtful, more loving spouse.* Have you noticed, gentle reader, that I am directing you to concentrate on changing you?

3. *Learn to use I messages.* Be able to say, "I like it when you (whatever)" or "I feel disrespected when you (whatever)." This is a helpful, non-blaming way to express appreciation for what our spouses do that we like and to ask for changes in what they do that bothers or hurts us. Of course, even the most respectful, non-blaming communication in the world doesn't guarantee we'll get what we request.

4. *Get help to change abusive patterns in your marriage.* Scripture commands us to separate ourselves from

"deeds of darkness" and to purposefully expose them. (See Eph. 5:11.) Such deeds include spouse abuse as well as child abuse. (I'll say more about the child abuse in Chapter 16.) In extreme cases you may need to consider separating with the goal of working toward reconciliation. Perhaps an entirely new, healthier foundation needs to be established.

5. *Never pursue divorce until you have worked hard in counseling, exhausted all possibilities, and see that your spouse intends to repeatedly, unrepentently desecrate and desert his or her marital commitment.* God does not ask you to give your life or the lives of your children to save your spouse, as some dangerously unbiblical Christian "helpers" often tell spouses in genuinely life-threatening marriages. God has already sent Jesus to lay down his life to save your spouse. If battering spouses aren't moved to repentance by Jesus' death, why would anyone think they would be won to the Lord by your death, or your child's? God hates divorce. God hates oppression of the less powerful, too. If churches would apply biblical guidelines for disciplining clearly abusive spouses, and for helping the victimized as well as the victimizers, there would be far less of both.

Relational Wounds Healing Overview
and Progress Evaluation

KEY ISSUES	SEEING TRUTH	NEW CHOICES	NEW PRACTICING
Personal Boundary Styles in Relating	I've been too "open" or too "closed" as a way of keeping myself safe	Try out a more balanced personal boundary style with my safest friends	Use a more balanced personal boundary style in all my relationships
Personal Responsibility Styles in Relating	I've been using "over-" or "under-" responsibility as a defense	Try out a more balanced responsibility style to find those who also seek mutuality	Relating consistently with mutual responsibility and biblical one-anothering
Leaving and Cleaving	I haven't transferred primary loyalty from parents to spouse	Identify marital problems related to my loyalty conflicts	Consistently put my spouse and his/her needs and desires ahead of parents'

Pause to Ponder and Pray

PONDER: Use the H.O.P.E. chart to get an idea of where you are in your changing and healing process in the area of interpersonal relationships.

✔ Use the Relational Rectangle with your spouse to evaluate your marriage.

✔ Share your observations with your spouse after asking him or her to share his or hers with you.

PRAY: Lord, please help me see and begin making the changes I need to make to have the kind of relationships you describe in your word. This is really difficult, so thank you for promising to be all I need to do what you call me to do. Amen.

Just Ahead

As we've seen in this chapter, interpersonal relationships are emotional mine fields. Certainly this holds true in relationships between leaders and followers. We'll look into that next.

CHAPTER
Ten

Help for
Healing Leaders

"Don't be alarmed, but someone is following you!"

Someone follows me too, because I'm a leader and so are you. Of course, we're also followers. I don't know which of those two ideas you struggle with more, but I ask you to consider that both are true.

In this chapter, I'll highlight a few of the special challenges and pitfalls we face as leaders. In the next chapter we'll look at the business of being followers. While most of what I'll cover is applicable in employer-employee and other power differential relationships, our focus here will be primarily church and parachurch leaders.

Hurt Leaders Hurt More People

Each of us has some sphere of influence where we lead. Granted some of our influence spheres are larger and some of our leadership positions more public than others. You may be a "platform person," for example, speaking to large audiences, or you might be a full-time homemaker influencing preschoolers. Whatever your present place in life, in some way you lead as well as follow.

If it's true that all of us are hurting and hurtful people, then potentially, at least, hurt people with more power and influence hurt more people.

If, as leaders, our levels of unseen wounds and power are high, but our levels of commitment to God-directed self-awareness and truthfulness are low, we are extremely dangerous people. Perhaps that sounds a little melodramatic, but I sincerely believe it's true. I've seen many loose-cannon leaders wound a lot of people, and I still have scars from some of the shrapnel.

Sadly, some leaders are unwilling to do the difficult, painful change work necessary to reduce their unseen wounds by increasing their God-given self-awareness and truthfulness. In each case, others with more power and authority need to intervene to significantly reduce the unwilling leader's level of power and influence. When this happens in business and industry, the extreme form is called unemployment. In Christian circles, we know it as church discipline.

God knew that churches filled with hurting, hurtful people would need these interventions, so he provided guidelines in Scripture. (See Matt. 18:15–17 and 1 Cor. 5:1–5.) God also graciously provides direction for restoration, when the sincerely repentant and significantly healed leader has genuinely changed.

Why would we need to be concerned about leaders' potentials to deeply wound great numbers of people and why would God put guidelines for church discipline in Scripture? Why doesn't God just call completely safe, totally trustworthy, and perfectly non-wounding people into leadership roles? (Unfortunately, many of us followers think he does. We'll talk more about that in Chapter 12.)

God uses weak, wounding, needy, hurting, hurtful people like you and me for his purpose in small and great ways because he doesn't have any other kind! No other species of humans exists, at least not on this planet. This means that the question about our wounds is not *if* we'll have them, but *where* they'll be, *what kinds* of wounds we'll have, and *how deep* the scars will go. It's when we forget this truth, whether we are leading or following, that we are most dangerous and most vulnerable.

What are the telltale marks of leaders who are likely to be especially hurtful to their followers? The signs include authority approval confusion, conflict about having fans or friends and family, and pedestal-preserving compromise.

Authority Approval Confusion

Did you hear the story about the father and son who were leading their donkey to market? Someone said they were dumb to walk while leading a strong animal. So they rode a while until someone else accused them of animal cruelty, saying, "That poor beast is too small for both of you." They got off and the dad told his son to ride for a while. The boy did until someone else said the lad was disrespecting his poor old father. So the father rode the donkey until another passerby noticed that the boy looked weary, and scolded the father for not letting his son ride.

When last seen, father and son were both walking and carrying the donkey!

I've carried some pretty heavy donkeys in my day. How about you? Leaders usually do a lot of donkey carrying, or the equivalent, when they're trying to please everybody. While that goal is unrealistic, it is not unusual for hurting leaders to want everyone to love them.

Am I implying that insecure, approval-seeking leaders might choose to pander to their followers or congregations, rather than risk rejection and losing their influential positions? Yes, indeed. I think this issue relates directly to the question of whose approval we seek when we serve, lead, help, counsel, and/or minister. The answer depends on whose servants we are.

"My ministry is just to help and serve people all I can in whatever humble little way the Lord provides."

What's your first impression of this statement made by a handsome, eloquent, fortyish senior pastor of a large South-

ern church? He sounds pretty good, doesn't he? Look and
listen again. Whose servant is this fellow? By his own
admission he serves the congregation, the church board, and
the television audience that watches his weekly worship
service broadcast.

There are many reasons for not becoming enslaved to other
people as their approval-seeking servants. Two stand out.
First, the "leader" will burn out faster than you can say
nervous breakdown. Just consider how pastoral roles have
multiplied in recent years. Different folks want their spiritual leaders to do different things. Since most churches in
America have only one pastor, he or she must manage somehow to fill many different roles.

In large, multi-staff congregations, expectations for leaders can be astonishingly unrealistic and wounding. A friend
of mine is an outstanding leader in the area of Christian
recovery. He is a successfully recovering alcoholic, an ordained minister, a gifted communicator, an effective counselor, and has authored several books. One of Southern
California's largest, most recovery-oriented churches con-
tacted him to become its Recovery Pastor. (To fully appreci-
ate this story, you have to remember that one of the hall-
marks of the recovery movement—whether Christian or secular—is balanced, healthy living.) Written into the Recovery
Pastor's contract and job description was the number of hours
this dear guy was expected to work each week. Keeping in
mind that this church wanted my friend to lead folks away
from addictive lifestyles toward balanced, healthy living,
guess how many hours they wanted him to work every week.
Fifty! That's right—fifty! They wanted him to contract to live
a work-focused, unbalanced, unhealthy lifestyle while teaching recovery! If this church had the temerity to write fifty
hours a week into his contract, imagine how many unwritten
extra hours he would likely have needed to work. He, his
wife, and I practically rolled on the floor with laughter as they
told me this story. But actually it isn't funny at all.

More importantly, if we serve others primarily, we will look
primarily to others for approval. Instead of fixing our eyes on
Jesus, as Hebrews 12:2 tells us to do, we will focus our gaze

on others to see how well we're doing. There's a verse tucked away in the Old Testament book of Jeremiah that scores a bull's-eye on this issue. God told his newly called prophet: "Do not be afraid of their faces, / For I am with you to deliver you" (1:8).

I wonder if Jeremiah might have been vulnerable to the approval addiction that makes us scrutinize our approval dispensers' faces for the tiniest nuances of disagreement or disapproval. When we do that we can instantly adjust our appearance or our words or do whatever it takes until once again we can relax in the chilling warmth of their affirming nods and smiles. I'm just guessing of course, but I surely understand fear of faces. How about you?

A few years ago, God used John 12:43 to nail my hide to the wall about this approval-addiction business. In this verse Jesus describes the religious leaders of his day as people who love the approval of other people more than God's. When I read this verse, I felt like I'd taken a bullet in the heart! Actually "the sword of the Spirit"—God's Word—pierced my inordinate adoration of others' affirmations.

"Willard, I'm starting to question your interpretation of those passages about submission."

When our senses of identity and worth depend on other people's approval, we focus on and tune in to *their* words more than *God's* word. For example, some Christian men do not want to be reminded that Scripture denounces victimization of the less powerful, but they want frequent sermons on submission. If such men happen to be the most powerful, influential approval-dispensers in the church, an approval-addicted pastor will likely follow their wishes. Consequently he or she would actually support unbalanced, unbiblical interpretations of Scripture that produce marriages which are nearly as unhealthy as the one depicted in the previous cartoon. The really scary part is that usually they won't even know they are choosing to do it!

And they and we also might not know we choose fans instead of friends or family.

Fans or Friends and Family?

A therapist friend, Tom Barrett, lives near Washington, D.C., and counsels with a number of government officials. His observations about these officials' public-life versus private-life struggles apply to us unofficial types, too.

Tom has noticed that many public-focused platform-people seem to want fans more than friends, respect more than relationships, and influence more than intimacy.

The independent ministries and Christian businesses that have multiplied in recent decades have created arenas where such preference for unreal, facade-to-facade interactions abound. Mark, an evangelical ex-entrepreneur, knows about this firsthand.

"I really thought I was cranking for the Lord, you know. I mean people poured into my conferences, bought my tapes and manuals, and told me I was great. The tighter my schedule and the greater my responsibilities, the more new people I met who almost always thought I was great. I never bothered putting together a board of directors or really connecting with a church to provide any sort of oversight. I didn't want anyone getting too close or too involved in my ministry."

Little by little, Mark relied more and more on his "standard stuff," as he called it. And little by little, his spiritual and moral life went down the tubes.

Mark was a smile-flashing, blow-dried, likable young Christian. He was also a refugee from a hurtful family. He preferred a bump-and-run relational style that never let anyone get too close. Candidly sharing his struggles with or seeking honest opinions from others just never made Mark's list of priorities. He made the same mistake that many Marks and Mark-followers make. He confused popular success and a higher bank balance with divine blessing. It's easy to forget that God is the one we are to please, not the paying public or our accountants.

Many of us hurting, hurtful people need to ask God to search our hearts and show us if we value fans kept at arm's length over friends who are close enough to see our flaws. That kind of wisdom is likely to be in our hidden parts. We also could ask someone in our families. Try a spouse for a really honest answer, because preferring impersonal relationships with adoring fans has an enormous impact on our families.

Public Versus Home Conflict

We don't have to be pastors, government officials, bosses, or famous in any way to wrestle with a preference for public life. Full-time homemakers, for example, who get involved in church or community volunteer work at whatever level of leadership, are just as likely to find their identities in those activities as more prominent platform-people and pulpit leaders are to find their identities in their endeavors.

The more performance-based our self-concepts, the more we tend to focus on our highest profile activities (whether paid or volunteer). And let's face it, most "at home" stuff is pretty low profile from the world's point of view.

This chart is my summary of Tom Barrett's observations about this public-life versus home-life struggle.[1]

Summary of Public-Life vs. Home-Life Conflict

IN PUBLIC	AT HOME
Treated like Superperson/hero People are sensitive to my needs Expected to help change the world	Treated like Clark Kent/ordinary person People expect me to be sensitive to their needs Expected to change light bulbs, diapers, etc.

Tom suggests that if public performance-focused spouses or parents put their families' unwritten contracts in print, some of the following would be included.

Public Performer's Family Contract

- We understand that I and my public performances are more important than anyone or anything else in this family.

- We understand that I will be preoccupied with giving my all to my public performance.

- We understand that I need to hear of your support, but not your struggles.

- We understand that all of you are essentially on your own.

- We understand that you are expected to totally deny all of your personal needs for as long as you can and maybe even longer.

Signatures: _____ _____
                              (Husband)   (Wife)

_____ _____
                 (Child)   (Child)

What happens to people with public performance and platform orientations that makes them favor fans over friends and bail out on their spouses and children? I think the answer is different in each situation, but I expect a common thread is woven through all these hurting folks and their hurting families. The public person gets seduced by the pedestal lifestyle.

Pedestal-Preserving Compromise

Pedestals are very precarious places for human beings because God didn't design us to perch and posture on pedestals. I am using pedestal-posturing as a synonym for looking perfect and problem-free. But when we cooperate with those who seek to put us on pedestals, we are colluding in the perpetration of fraud. And that's a crime both legally and spiritually.

Can you see why shame-wounded adults gravitate toward pedestals? When we are shame-wounded we think we must be perfect to earn a place on this planet. People get pedestalized when they go along with other shame-bound people who expect their leaders to be perfect. But since human beings are not perfect that means that pedestal people inevitably compromise the truth and develop secret lives.

The Secret-Life Syndrome

Do you remember the image on Ted Koppel's TV program, "Nightline," of a leading televangelist, Jimmy Swaggart, calling another leading televangelist, Jim Bakker, a "cancer in the body of Christ"? I vividly recall Swaggart looking and sounding genuinely appalled at Bakker's newly revealed secret life of sexual sin. What we didn't know at the time was that Swaggart himself was caught up in the Secret-Life Syndrome.

Jimmy Swaggart is simply the best-known of a host of public-performing platform people trapped in the devastating double bind of pedestal lifestyles. The majority of these wounded and wounding leaders, no doubt including Swaggart, never meant to live secret lives but they are the direct result of their allowing themselves to be pedestalized.

Suppose, as an example, a man habitually visits pornography shops and prostitutes. He probably loathes himself for this, vowing with each visit to try harder to stop. I've even heard of people going into religious work so they would *have* to stop committing some despised but life-dominating sin. By preaching and teaching against such behavior, and being aware of the need to model godly living, they hope to paint themselves into a moral corner, so to speak.

Apparently, these deluded leaders trust other people's expectations of them to control their out-of-control behavior. This is simply magical thinking. And, because magical thinking denies reality, it always leads to more hurt, not less. The really painful part of this double bind is that pedestalized leaders believe they cannot admit the truth about their imperfect, out-of-control lives and reach out and get help. They are trapped on their pedestals with their secret lives, pretending that Christian leaders are perfect.

A recent issue of *Christianity Today* reported that a sixty-five-year-old Episcopal charismatic leader had been relieved of duties. This man had admitted to "homosexual liaisons, some with counselees, over the past two decades." One of the saddest, and most telling, aspects of the article was what the fallen leader said. According to the report:

> [This man] who is married with six children said he is "deeply ashamed and totally guilty of what I did." He said he had been "tormented" by homosexuality since his teens, but that disappeared when he became a charismatic in 1964. Some time later, he said, he lapsed into homosexual practice.[2]

Did you catch it? He sincerely believed his tormenting problem "disappeared" when he had a deep spiritual experience. But it didn't. This leader apparently bought into the pedestal-person lie that he had to be perfect or his Christian experience would be in doubt. This leader and his Episcopal diocese deserve credit for admitting and addressing the problem. Many leaders and their superiors never do.

Trust Bandits and Sexual Misconduct

This desperately sad situation lends credence to the 1988 study by *Leadership* magazine indicating that of the approximately three hundred pastors who responded to a questionnaire (of the one thousand surveyed) most indicated that sexual temptation and infidelity were significant concerns. When ministers become sexually involved with congregants who come to them for pastoral counseling, the betrayal of trust is devastating beyond description. I've counseled many women who were victimized this way.

"But, Sandy, those are adolescent or young adult women, not little girls," you may be thinking. "They're just as responsible for what happened as the minister." At first glance, that seems a reasonable rationale for evaluating responsibility in such cases. Certainly when this type of situation becomes known in churches, most members are quicker to blame the woman for seducing the pastor than to hold him responsible. I think that perception has basic flaws. Consider what David Johnson, a senior pastor, and Jeff VanVonderen, an ordained minister and the counseling pastor in the church where they co-pastor, say about a situation of this kind:

> Even if she did try to seduce him, while that would have been immoral, what he did was illegal. Her behavior would not justify his. There is no legal reason for a pastor to become sexually involved with a counselee. *Someone* is supposed to be the healthy person. Shouldn't it be the spiritual helper?[3]

Because such hurtful spiritual "helpers" represent God, their rapes of the trust counselees or congregants bestow on them is blatant spiritual abuse. But when these helpers are leaders in large, financially successful churches, such abuse may go unnoticed by all but the victims.

Success and Secrets

In unhealthy organizations, either religious or secular, small, inner circles of people who ignore and even suppress the truth often surround the leaders to perform damage-control duty when a leader's secret life begins to spring leaks. The media gleefully reported just such a situation in both the Bakker and Swaggart cases. It's as if adultery, tax evasion, lack of integrity don't matter so long as nobody finds out and those cards and letters keep coming in—preferably with generous checks enclosed.

These leaders and groups specialize in camouflaging their motives and methods by developing great fluency in what I call "secret speak." They use language to obfuscate the truth rather than to communicate it.

Proverbs 18:21 clearly describes the enormous influence of words. It says that "death and life are in the power of the tongue." "They call good evil and evil good" is how the Bible describes the rationalizing of corrupt leaders. Talk about the relevance of Scripture! And talk about the devastating wounds that will result in those who trusted such untrustworthy, truth-twisting leaders!

Wilson's Law of Behavior Selection says, *If you have to lie about it, don't do it.* Following this law would prevent mountains of misery for millions of followers, and their leaders, too. As always, truth is what makes us free, even though it sometimes makes us angry and miserable.

We all long for the complete eradication of sin and the blissful, perfect peace that state would bring to our lives. But our believing that we have arrived at that longed-for state is consummate self-deception. And, as we've seen, self-deceived people in positions of leadership are profoundly dangerous and hurtful. There is, however, an antidote to the self-deception and pitfalls of trying to live on a pedestal.

Humble Self-Suspicion

J. I. Packer coined the phrase "humble self-suspicion" to describe the reality cure many Christians need to correct their skewed views of spirituality. Packer believes that many sincere believers are too quick to testify to being wholly holy and spiritually well. He suggests that the spiritual health we proclaim is partial and relative when measured by the absolute standard of spiritual health we see in Jesus.[4]

Let's give God glory that we are less spiritually sick and incapacitated today than we were yesterday. But let's stay real! This means staying off both large and small pedestals and telling the truth about our flaws, failures, and ongoing struggles to live authentically for Christ. This also means remaining humbly self-suspicious and self-aware. We ought to anticipate, rather than be shocked by, our lust for pedestals and the acclaim of admiring friends who too quickly can become adoring followers. The more we recognize our susceptibility to such seductive circumstances, the safer and more trustworthy we are, whatever our spheres of influence.

What is the secret to keeping our balance and being less hurtful leaders? It is knowing that the greatest danger for any of us is forgetting that all of us have limitations and are still imperfect and sinful. Dr. Archibald Hart said it well: "Christian leaders don't fall because they forget they are holy, they fall because they forget they are human."[5]

Specific Change Strategies

We need to remind ourselves that each of us is a leader to someone, even though that idea seems unlikely to some of us. So the following suggestions can benefit all of us.

1. *Honestly assess the level of binding shame in your belief system.* When we still function from a shame grid in much of our lives, we are sitting ducks for the leader struggles we've examined. When we're shame-bound, we'll always feel we have to work twice as hard to be half as good as others. And when we believe we don't deserve our leadership positions, especially in Christian ministry, we may actually sabotage ourselves without even realizing it. Remember, everything about the Christian pilgrimage is about God's grace. Accept whatever place of service God gives you with humility and gratitude for his grace.

2. *Take time to rest.* This is a key to avoiding a three-alarm burnout. Leaders teetering on the edge of burnout— whether homemakers or pastors—usually spend too much time and emotional energy caring for others and too little caring for themselves. At those times, I've been far too tired for a mere coffee break. I needed a psychotic break! That happens when we attempt to out-work and under-rest everyone we know, including Jesus. Luke 5:15–16 says: "Yet the news about him spread all the more, so that crowds of people came to hear him and to be healed of their sicknesses. But Jesus often withdrew to lonely places and prayed" (NIV).
   Did you catch the words *often withdrew*? I honestly doubt that a lot of today's churches would hire Jesus if his work habits were well-known. Certainly he

wouldn't have been offered the Recovery Pastor's position at that large Southern California church that was pursuing my friend.

Sometimes the Christians who talk the most about Jesus' being our supreme example (which, of course, he is) are the very folks least likely to follow his often-withdrew-to-lonely-places-and-prayed example.

3. *Evaluate your susceptibility to pedestalization and the Secret-Life Syndrome.* If you struggle with approval addiction as I do, you may be craving virtual adoration to compensate for the affirmation deprivation of your childhood. When this is the case, we are apt to seek followers and fans who see us as more than we are or ever can be, instead of friends who know us "warts and all," so to speak. This is dangerous and destructive for us as well as for our followers and our friends.

4. *Develop a Circle of Safety for accountability.* Without implementing this fourth strategy, it is doubtful whether we can consistently practice the other three. This accountability relationship is an absolute, nonnegotiable must for everyone at any level of ministry of any kind. Period. It is nearly that critical for all the rest of us. For those circles of safety, we need at least two or three ruthlessly honest folks who love us a lot and Jesus far more. Such relationships help us flee temptations (sexual and otherwise) and avoid self-deception about our unlimited capacities to do and be everything to everyone. This will help us stay off pedestals, escape burnout, and maintain balanced lives.

Leader's Wounds H.O.P.E. Chart

KEY ISSUES	SEEING TRUTH	NEW CHOICES	NEW PRACTICING
Seeking approval from God, not Others	I've been living more for the approval of people than for God's	Choosing what I do/say to please God, even when it's not popular	Putting more God-pleasing choices in more areas of my life
Having Family/Friends, not Fans/Followers	Admit I prefer high profile positions that make me feel big	Purposely take "off the pedestal" positions more often	Being comfortable in both low and high profile roles
Accountability to avoid Secret-Life Syndrome	I am at risk for the Secret-Life Syndrome	Identify and engage the people who can provide accountability	Meeting often and being real with my accountability group

---

Pause to Ponder and Pray

PONDER: Use the H.O.P.E. chart to find where you are in your changing and healing process regarding leadership wounds.

✔ You might want to review Appendix B to recall your true identity in Christ. The more we believe about ourselves what God believes about us, the less we'll need to posture on pedestals pandering for approval.

PRAY: Lord, please help me hold with an open hand and a heart of gratitude whatever positions of leadership you've given me. And as I do it, please help me keep my eyes on you. Amen.

Just Ahead

I began this chapter by suggesting that we are all leaders *and* followers. Each role holds its own set of challenges for hurting people. We've looked a bit at leaders' issues, so it's the followers' turn next.

CHAPTER
Eleven

Help for
Healing Followers

"I can hardly wait to see what I'll be when I grow up."

I laughingly but semi-seriously say that as I ponder my delayed adolescence, which began at about age thirty-five. A most difficult aspect of my reluctant maturity involved what many hurting followers need to do—grow up enough to stop viewing our leaders through rose-colored glasses.

I'll confess that I've been guilty of pedestalizing leaders in my earlier, more gullible, naive days. How about you?

I sort of skipped and giggled my Mary Poppins way through relationships with people in positions of authority. My husband used to tell me that I lived in a Sunday school world because I assumed that everyone was sweet and sincere. I wore my naiveté like a shiny badge of honor and thought Garth was being terribly cynical. Well, my naiveté badge tarnished quite some time ago. Now I think that Garth was far closer to the truth than I was back in my rose-colored glasses days.

As followers, not only must we maintain self-awareness and humble self-suspicion regarding ourselves, but also we need to cultivate a similar approach to others, including those who would be our leaders. Does that sound too cynical and somewhat unChristian? Take a moment and turn to 1 John 4:1. That verse is God's call to ruthless realism regarding spiritual leaders: "Beloved, do not believe every spirit, but test the spirits, whether they are of God; because many false prophets have gone out into the world." Clearly, God doesn't want us to gullibly swallow everything we hear from every person who claims to represent Jesus Christ.

Why are we so often drawn to people who falsely make that claim? I think it has something to do with our gullibility training in hurtful families and the incredibly deceitful disguises hurtful leaders often wear.

Set-ups for Follower Wounds

When we stop to think about it, hurting and hurtful families are perfect prep schools for our later participation in unhealthy organizations. Growing up in these families, we become champion secret-keepers and people-pleasers. Such families' rules teach children to accept their leaders'—parents'—views of reality without seeing, let alone talking about, more truthful views. So we adult children from hurtful families usually have only a vague idea of what constitutes appropriate relationships. This is an important issue when we consider some of the data about leaders' misconduct.

Discussing the fact that churches are beginning to be more conscious of personal boundary issues, a professor at a Midwestern seminary said, "Churches are so much [more] aware of the violations of boundaries, especially with regard to sexual boundaries, that this has created all kinds of havoc and confusion. It reveals that there are many people who, because of the family of origin or whatever, simply are not clear about what's appropriate and inappropriate."[1]

As we learn more about healthy relationships and personal boundaries, we are better prepared to evaluate authority figures' attitudes and actions toward us. Too often, though, we wounded followers get re-wounded.

Deception and Destruction

In addition to our early gullibility training in unhealthy families, the sheer magnitude of deception employed by many spiritual leaders is mind-blowing.

Recently a leading denominationally affiliated university relieved a Christian ethics professor of his duties because of sexual misconduct with eight women. Reading about that incident reminded me of a story I had read only days before about Reuben Sturman, the man *Time* magazine dubbed America's "Porn King."

This guy reportedly grosses one million dollars a day from the sale of magazines and videos that include bestiality and child pornography. (That's right, *one million dollars!*) Reading this article a casual observer could conclude that Mr. Sturman is deeply committed to cleanliness. It said, "Sturman [is] a cleanliness freak who [always wears] a surgical mask,"[2] and the magazine included a photo of this filth merchant wearing his surgical mask to validate the man's obsession with cleanliness.

In my opinion, this porn king wearing his surgical mask is no more bizarre than a Christian ethics professor making sexual advances. Either situation stands reality on its head. Both illustrate a popular tactic employed by deceitful leaders who wear disguises that are absolutely opposite of their true inner-heart attitudes.

This kind of high-handed deception is why God instructed us to test the spirits of spiritual authority figures. However, we easily overlook this admonition when we long deeply for approval from precisely these people. And it's very likely that we will if we've grown up in families that tutored us in perfectionistic performing to earn approval.

Authority Figure Approval Addiction

Only in the past few years have I recognized that the particular focus of my approval addiction centers on winning the approval of men in positions of perceived authority. Note the word *perceived*—that's a key to the subjectivity of this whole thing. I may perceive someone as an authority figure, while you may see him or her as a peer, as a subordinate, or as a jerk. I'm embarrassed that it took me so long to see this when now it seems so obvious. Because I didn't have a healthy male authority figure while I was growing up, I entered adulthood ripe for my particular style of approval addiction.

What's your style? From whom do you most long to win a smile? It may seem very simplistic, but I really believe our particular approval addictions have a lot to do with the relationships we had with our parents when we were young. Check it out in your own life. This issue daily becomes more relevant because of the increasing phenomenon known as "father loss." (I was a trendsetter without knowing it.)

Many adults rightfully labeled "workaholics" are literally killing themselves, and often sacrificing their families in the process, to gain approval from male bosses. Their need for this approval far outweighs their desire for fatter paychecks, loftier titles, or bigger offices. When this happens, the father-starved workers, whether in secular or religious organizations, are sitting ducks for authority abuse.

If you are, or ever have been, one of these employees, you'll identify with the sentiments expressed in the following sign:

WE APPROVAL-SEEKING WORKAHOLICS
ARE KILLING OURSELVES DOING THE
IMPOSSIBLE FOR THE UNGRATEFUL.
WE HAVE DONE SO MUCH WITH SO LITTLE
FOR SO LONG,
WE ARE NOW QUALIFIED TO DO ANYTHING
WITH NOTHING!

It's easy to see that this addiction to the approval of authority figures, who may or may not be substitute fathers, breeds a love for the approval of human beings that can surpass love for God's approval. You'll remember that this was Jesus' scathing indictment of contemporary religious leaders. By the way, those people loved to make disciples.

Whose Disciples?

Deeply wounded, empty-feeling adolescents and adults often mistakenly turn to appealing, powerful leaders to find fulfillment. This phenomenon fuels religious groups from mainline evangelical to fringe churches and outright cults. Jesus calls us to be true disciples, or learners, and he promises to fully satisfy all who answer his call. But sometimes it seems that instead of becoming disciples of our Lord, we become *disciples of disciples*. We shame-bound spiritual seekers struggle with believing God would ever deal with us directly and personally through Jesus. Consequently we attach ourselves to someone we think is "good enough" to merit such direct and personal connection. We just try to stay close enough to catch some of the spiritual crumbs a good-enough-for-Jesus disciple might throw us. Unfortunately, some of the men and women we pedestalize dispense some pretty crummy, even terribly toxic, spiritual teaching.

Whose Truth?

Recently I saw the Public Broadcasting System's moving special, "Children of Chernobyl." A narrator described the nuclear cloud that passed directly over the large city of Kiev on May 1, less than a week following the tragedy. Since officials chose to withhold warnings from the residents of Kiev, hundreds of thousands of adults and children stood in the streets for hours watching a May Day parade at exactly the time their exposure to nuclear fallout was at its worst.

The reporter asked a Kiev mother, whose child was dying from cancer, what she was told when she and others expressed concern after learning about their exposure. Her astounding reply was, "We were told to close our windows and wash our hair."

By the time the special was filmed, scientists had calculated that the children who were downwind of Chernobyl after the disaster occurred had a 250 percent higher risk of cancer than before the nuclear accident. (The adult cancer rate rose 80 percent.) Closing one's windows and washing one's hair would not appear to prevent the damage official statements worked so hard to deny!

The television special noted that when one of Kiev's citizens asked for a Geiger counter to measure radiation, the government's official response was, "Why do you want to cause trouble? You don't need a Geiger counter. Everything is all right." That sounds vaguely familiar, doesn't it?

The person who sees and describes the problem becomes the problem in truth-fearing organizations. A question like, "Why do you want to cause trouble?" is a classic example of how a person in authority within an abusive, secret-supporting system responds to the threat of truth.

This can happen in churches, too! Many abusive, truth-fearing churches seem to teach that "niceness" is better for the church family than honesty. They're wrong. "Nice" is not even listed as a fruit of the Spirit in Galatians 5:22–23. That's a real shocker to some Christians! It was to Claudia.

I met Claudia at a conference in California. An exquisitely groomed, middle-aged woman, she told me about her anguish at recently changing churches after years of soul-searching and prayer. "Every time I tried to talk to any leaders or staff members about my concern at what I saw in the youth program, I was told to 'think on these things of what's kind and lovely.' I heard that Philippians 4 passage quoted so often, I decided I'd better go before the Lord with it in front of me, and ask him for guidance."

Claudia did just that and discovered that the Scripture fragment used to squelch her concerns had been twisted to suit the purposes of the appearance-preserving church staff. Philippians 4:8 actually begins: "Finally, brothers, whatever is true" (NIV), and then lists other qualities such as noble, admirable, and excellent, before exhorting believers to "think about such things." Somehow Claudia's church staff had overlooked the very first thing God wants us to think about—truth.

By the way, Claudia's perceptions proved accurate. About six months after she left that church, one of the youth pastors was dismissed and subsequently charged with sexual misconduct with a minor. She told me this with tears. Wouldn't it be shocking if some pastors preached what they practice? And these religious trust bandits are supposed to represent God!

Sometimes though, Christ's undershepherds—pastors— are battered and bloodied by their sheep! I know of church boards who have abused hurt and struggling pastors when they tried to walk in truth. For instance, instead of supporting their pastor's honest acknowledgment of personal and church problems and his desire to get help, one elder board ordered him to resign. They threatened to withhold severance pay unless he "left quietly," saying he would "split the church" or at the least "cause problems" if he told the truth. These elders forgot that "the truth is *never* the problem. The problem is *always* the problem."[3]

Then there are the churches where sexually abusing leaders are quietly transferred to other unsuspecting congregations, while the courageous whistle-blower is browbeaten into silence. Even more evil, perhaps, are churches where sexually abusing leaders hide behind such poisonous perversions of Scripture as "touch not God's anointed," while accusing their truth-telling victims of seduction and stirring up strife. In such unhealthy and unholy situations, the abuser usually remains in his position of trust, influence, and authority, while the victim is put out of the church.

What's Wrong With This Picture?

Do you recall seeing drawings with one object completely out of place with the rest of the scene? It might be a jungle scene with a bicycle perched in a banyan tree that asks, "What's wrong with this picture?" Obviously, the bicycle in the banyan tree is what's wrong.

The church is the one and only system founded by Jesus who called himself Truth. Therefore, I believe he would declare that exalting reputation over character, public impression over personal integrity, and image over truth is what's wrong with the picture in his church. But be warned: lovers of truth pay a price in truth-fearing groups. Truth-noticing followers who question their religious leaders' conduct often hear themselves accused of being judgmental. This is the evangelicalized version of the secular accusation of intolerance.

In the confusion about individuals' rights, we may sacrifice our responsibility to evaluate the acts of others on the altar of unlimited tolerance and indiscriminate compassion. We live in a society where tolerance has become our highest value, far more prized than individual responsibility or truth. Some of us are, or have been, in religious systems that hold the same inverted, unbiblical values. I think this would make Jesus weep. (See Rev. 3:16 for Jesus' reaction to moral and spiritual lukewarmness or truthless tolerance.)

On the other hand, truth-seeing and truth-speaking followers may be told they don't know enough—certainly not as much as their leaders—therefore, they have no business questioning the leaders' doctrines or directions.

John, the beloved disciple, wrote that every Christian has the same divine anointing that enables us to learn from God so that no one of us needs to depend totally upon human teachers for spiritual truth. (See 1 John 2:27.) God never tells us to shift our brains into neutral and coast spiritually, while others steer our spiritual lives.

Where's the Exit?

What if you've inadvertently become involved with one of these power abusing, unhealthy religious systems with perfection-pretending, pedestal-posturing leaders because you "feel so at home" there? Can you get out? Yes, but usually not without suffering enormous pain for being the equivalent of the dysfunctional family's disloyal child. In dysfunctional *religious* families we're more apt to be called "apostate" or "backslidden." Occasionally, while we're still part of an unhealthy religious system, a leader's secret life will come to light and he or she will repent. We still need to be discerning and "test the spirit" of the repenter.

Where's the Repentance?

With unswerving consistency, God says that his focus is on our hearts and inner lives. His attitude toward repentance is no exception.

Scripture describes two types of repentance, or admission of sin. Both are summarized in Joel 2:13. One type is "rending our hearts." The other kind is called "rending our garments." The first is a very personal, internal decision known only to the repenter and God. In contrast, the second is a very public, external demonstration observed by dozens or, these days, even millions of people.

I can still see the televangelist with a multimillion following and budget, holding a microphone in one hand and dramatically raising the other heavenward as he contorted his face and ever so slowly intoned, "I have sinned." This example suggests how we can tell which type of repentance is which. That televangelist, Jimmy Swaggart, refused to submit to his denominational leaders when they imposed extremely reasonable guidelines for discipline and restoration. Sadly, he was later arrested for the same sexual sin that cracked his facade in the first place.

Sadly too, Swaggart demonstrates the wounding capacity of shame-bound thinking. For years, he told his viewing millions that no true Christian would ever *be* or *see* a counselor. Having publicly painted himself into the no-counseling-for-Christians corner, Swaggart apparently could not give himself permission to get the godly counsel he needed to understand and change his hurtful ways.

But I'm glad I know of "platform people" who have sincerely repented of sexual and other sins, sought and received help, and demonstrated the genuine "fruits of repentance" Scripture describes. We need to know about these cases. Otherwise we will become hopelessly disillusioned and give up on church and parachurch organizations altogether. Giving up is no more an answer than blind, mindless naiveté.

What is the secret to walking the tightrope between gullibility and cynicism? It is knowing that the greatest danger for all of us is forgetting that we are all imperfect, sinful human beings. Yet God mysteriously elects to work through people like us. Holding this reality clearly before us keeps us living in balanced interdependence with one another and in total dependence upon Christ. That's healthy for all of us leader/followers.

Specific Change Strategies

If we've been wounded in secular or religious organizations, we're likely to be angry at ourselves and shame ourselves for being "so stupid." That response only multiplies
our pain with self-inflicted wounds. Instead, try practicing
some of the following suggestions.

1. *Forgive yourself for being human.* Human beings get
   tricked, taken in, conned, duped, and deceived all the
   time, especially if they were schooled in early life to
   mindlessly accept leader-created realities. You might
   want to find a Christ-centered support group for adult
   children from hurtful families where you can safely
   share your pain. It's comforting to know we're not the
   only ones.

2. *Learn the biblical marks of an authentic and trustworthy
   leader.* Read the gospels, looking specifically at Jesus'
   leadership style. Although the apostle Paul was far from
   perfect, his leadership qualities, as described in the
   epistles, provide other helpful examples.
   The Old Testament book of Amos paints a word picture that's critical in discerning false leaders and
   teachings from genuine ones. In Amos 7:7–8 God tells
   his prophet that he's going to set a plumb line in the
   midst of his people. We who've wallpapered know the
   value of a plumb line, that pointed piece of lead tied
   to the end of a string that gives us the true vertical
   line we need to begin. God's Word is the only trustworthy plumb line of truth in the midst of this
   "crooked and perverse generation" in which we live.
   We must purposefully take the plumb line of Scripture
   and lay all leaders' teachings alongside it to see what
   does and does not square with God's true vertical.

3. *Give yourself permission to grieve your lost relationships.*
   The trauma of leaving hurtful groups and leaders is very
   real and very painful. We must allow ourselves to mourn
   the relationships that meant a lot to us despite how
   unbalanced and unhealthy they might have been. We

need to find some substantially healthy helpers to provide support and encouragement during such times.

When we've been deeply wounded in childhood and again in adult life by trusted authority figures, we usually need some counseling help to move through our pain into healing. Part of this process probably includes acknowledging that some of our present anguish stems from emotions we had in childhood but didn't have the freedom to feel or express.

This combination of old and new anger and grief can feel overwhelming at times. So at the risk of being annoyingly redundant, *please get help for yourself*. And remember, that doesn't mean you're weak. It means you're human. Human is how God created us.

Follower's H.O.P.E. Chart

KEY ISSUE	SEEING TRUTH	NEW CHOICES	NEW PRACTICING
"Testing" all that leaders say/teach	I am "set up" to believe all that leaders teach	Give myself permission to question/"test" all that leaders teach	Test all that leaders teach by comparing to Bible

Pause to Ponder and Pray

PONDER: Use the H.O.P.E. chart to find where you are in your changing and healing process in the area of followers' wounds.

✔ After reading this chapter, do you suspect that you may be in a truth-fearing religious or secular organization?

✔ Is there a truth-seeking, trustworthy person outside of this organization with whom you could discuss this?

If so, will you contact him/her to schedule such a discussion? When?

PRAY: Lord, please help me be willing to see the truth about the religious and secular leaders I've been believing and following. If necessary, give me the courage to leave whatever group I'm in that misrepresents truth. Thank you for your Word which provides the plumb line I need to measure all teachings. Amen.

Just Ahead

We don't need to be theologians to figure out that stumbling into religious groups led by deceitful leaders foreshadows spiritual abuse. In reality, even if we manage to avoid such groups and leaders, growing up in hurtful families is sufficient to produce deep spiritual wounds. That's our next topic.

CHAPTER
Twelve

Help for
Healing Worshipers

"God is like a Santa Claus who is known by everyone but not believed in by everyone. God brings special gifts to good people and tries to help the bad people. . . . God is the apple on the tree of life."[1]

This description of God came from several junior high-age children. Yet in a deeper sense, the word pictures of God came from their parents.

By now most of us have heard that our concepts of God directly relate to the kind of relationships we had with our earliest adult authority figures. We don't have to be theologians to figure out that this spells trouble for children raised in hurting and hurtful families. Actually, it spells S-P-I-R-I-T-U-A-L A-B-U-S-E.

All child abuse is spiritual abuse. Mistreating children through neglect or blatant abuse misrepresents the character and purposes of God, the ultimate authority figure. That creates confusion about God that can last a lifetime.

Confusion About God

We don't have to have been beaten or locked in closets to have distorted ideas about God. None of those things happened to Jeff, but his ideas were distorted just the same.

"I came from a faithful church-going home," Jeff told me in our first counseling session. This would-be seminarian described being raised by a morally clean, hard working, rigidly religious, demanding father and a passive, manipulative mother. The youngest of five children, Jeff knew at the age of six that he was an unwanted "accident." He overheard his mother say that in a conversation with her sister. "That was the moment I determined to make my mom and dad happy they had me. But no matter how hard I tried, I've never really felt I was good enough or that I did enough well enough to do that."

Jeff sought counseling because of what he heard me say in a seminar at our church. Specifically, he was concerned about entering seminary with his views of God as they were.

"I was so surprised when you said that God is not disappointed with us even though he's grieved about our sins. My problem isn't so much horrible sinning. Sure, I know I fail all the time and I confess it. But what bothers me most is that I always feel like God is really disappointed in me. Even my quiet times are never good enough."

As I gently probed for how this idea of God's disappointment affected him, Jeff's eyes began to glisten.

"I know that I really trusted Jesus as my Savior, but I keep wondering if I was *supposed* to. I know that sounds stupid, but I just keep wondering if God accepts me as his child even though I can't do everything as well as I wish I could."

I've met a lot of Jeffs through the years. I've been a bit of a Jeff, too, but my distorted deity was more a Demanding God.

Worshiper Wounds from Being Special

Most of my life I've worshiped a demanding deity who was never fully pleased with what I did, because he seemed to expect more from me than from his other children.

As well-meaning Christian parents often do, my mother used Scriptural support for her perfectionistic expectations of me. I can still hear her quoting from Luke 12:48: "From everyone who has been given much, much will be demanded" (NIV). That verse stirred a sense of gratitude for being "given much," while it generated guilt because so much more seemed to be required. I grew up deeply loving both God and my mother because they had given me so much. But I feared that I constantly disappointed them both because I could never fully satisfy their demands.

The year before she died of cancer at seventy-eight, my mother told me several times that she felt guilty for depriving me of a father. I think when I was a child, she tried to show me that, although I didn't have an earthly father to love me, my Heavenly Father proved he loved me by giving me special gifts—like being able to play the piano, sing, speak in public, and so forth. I believe she did this not only because she sincerely loved me, but also because it salved her painfully wounded self-concept to think that, from her perspective, she had borne a special child. Perhaps on some deep level she saw her supposedly special child as a sign that God was not angry about her failed first marriage.

Ironically, Mother was correct about how important earthly fathers are to children learning about their heavenly Father.

Father Wounds and Spiritual Confusion

Our parents' treatment of us in childhood, especially our fathers', significantly molded the concepts of God that shape and structure our present relationships with God. If I am correct about this, there is evidence of such a connection in our worship lives. The following exercise may supply some of that evidence.

On a piece of paper, or in your personal journal, briefly answer these questions about your father or the person(s) who filled the father-role in your childhood.[2]

- How close were you to your father (how approachable was he)?

- Did he show you that you were intrinsically valuable and unconditionally loved or did you have to perform in certain ways to earn his value and love?

- Did he have time for you? In other words, were you important enough to him to get his *appropriate* attention? (Sometimes, when fathers/parents spend time with their children, it is inappropriate and hurtful. For example, it is inappropriate for your father to spend time with you for his sexual gratification or as an excuse to get out of the house so he can drink.)

- Did he keep his promises (was he trustworthy)?

- Were you punished for being bad or disciplined in order to improve your character?

When you've finished answering these questions about your father, answer the same questions about God, using a separate page. When you finish answering the questions the second time, compare your responses. Do you see any similarities? No doubt you do, since fathers are powerful influences in their children's lives.

Fathers create their daughters' expectations about relationships with men in general and model for their sons what being masculine means. Fathers, even more than mothers, also create expectations about the treatment their children will receive from God. Perhaps this is why the heavenly-Parent-to-earthly-parents messages in Scripture are addressed to fathers. (See Eph. 6:4 and Col. 3:21.)

Fathers perform these functions even when they abandon their children by failing to maintain contact after divorce. These phantom fathers predispose their daughters to expect men to desert them. Their sons learn that when the going gets tough, real men get going—right out the door. Absentee dads teach all their children that God will abandon them just when they need him most.

No dad is perfect. Dads just need to be consistently adequate. But children who've been beaten, raped, constantly humiliated, rejected, and given only performance-based approval are apt to believe God will abuse and reject them, too. It's difficult to feel comfortable and enjoy being with someone we think has a club he's waiting to use on us or—at least—an ever lengthening list of demands we must fulfill perfectly before he'll accept us.

Fathers and the Oxymoron Effect

Fathers who neglect and/or abuse their offspring create what I call the Oxymoron Effect. As you'll recall, oxymorons are contradicting adjective-noun combinations like *fresh frozen*. We experience the Oxymoron Effect when biblically based descriptions of God seem contradictory.

Consider the term "loving father." We grasp the concept of *loving*, and we understand the meaning of *father*. But if our early experiences with our fathers or stepfathers significantly misrepresented God, combining those concepts creates spiritual confusion and contradiction—an oxymoron.

Many counselees describe the phenomenon this way: "I can't seem to connect to God the same way other Christians do. When I hear people pray to or talk about God as a 'loving father' something inside me freaks out. I want to jump up and scream, 'You've got to be kidding!'"

You may be shocked that genuinely born-again believers struggle with those and similar thoughts and feelings. Yet, many of you are those strugglers. When our parents significantly mispresented God, they opened the door to two major types of spiritual counterfeiting. Both are ancient lies that get repackaged for each new generation. And both versions of counterfeit spirituality relate directly to one's view of God's grace.

Counterfeit 1: No-Grace Theology

When it comes to God's grace—his unmerited favor toward his sinful human creatures—many "good" people basically say, "Thanks, but no thanks." The fatal flaw in no-grace theology is that, according to God himself, "There is no one righteous . . . no one who does good, not even one" (see Rom. 3:10–12, 23, NIV.) That doesn't mean people can't be nice and kind, even generous and compassionate. But it does mean that we can't "nice" our way into heaven.

Jesus dealt with the Pharisees, the official "good guys" of his day, by telling them that only the sick—not the healthy—need physicians and that he came to call sinners—not the righteous. (See Matt. 9:12–13.) His point to the no-grace good guys was that as long as they didn't recognize and acknowledge their sin-sickness, they wouldn't come to him, the Great Physician, for salvation and healing.

Some people adopt the no-grace counterfeit because they believe they are good enough *for* God. Others follow no-grace religions because they believe they are good enough to *be* God!

New Age No-Grace

Those of us with significant unseen wounds are sitting ducks for the modern version of no-grace because it promises inner healing. And who doesn't want some kind of inner healing? Today's religious gurus mix pop psychology and no-grace, "I am God," old-as-Eden, New Age spirituality in a nearly irresistible concoction lapped up by many sincerely seeking worshipers. One of the most revered New Age books, *A Course in Miracles*, is:

> a text and a workbook and manual with 365 lessons, one for each day. The faithful attend lectures and meditate. They also read from a Bible-like book said to have been dictated by "a voice" to an admitted atheist psychologist, named Helen Schucman, over seven years in the mid-1960s. . . . *The purpose: inner healing.*
>
> Ideas are based on universal spiritual themes, using Christian terms.[3]

Please notice the phrase "using Christian terms." That's what traps many spiritually hungry seekers into deceptive, disastrous counterfeits of genuine biblical Christianity. And what is the central message of "The Course"? According to the materials, the key to healing the human condition will come from our own hearts and minds.

That is reminiscent of something about "you shall be as gods," isn't it? New Age spirituality always keeps the no-need-for-God-or-his-grace concept of unlimited human potential at the heart of its twisted teachings. New Agers, however, aren't the only folks who twist spiritual truths. The other twist to counterfeit spirituality centers on a some-grace theology.

Counterfeit 2: Some-Grace Theology

As a kid, our son Dave latched onto the phrase "busy as a beaver." Eventually he shortened it to "beavering," as a synonym for working frantically.

I've spent a lot of time "beavering" for the Lord. How about you? That's fine as long as we're serving Christ from the overflow of our love-constrained, grace-grateful hearts. It's not so fine when we're beavering to earn enough good marks to outweigh our bad marks so we can guarantee our tickets to heaven or hedge against divinely designed disasters aimed in our directions.

Some-grace churches are filled with people beavering for the Lord. ("Beavering for the Lord" is a synonym for what I call "evangelical hyperactivity.") These busy churchgoers are descended from a long line of religious beaverers. Some of them received one of the apostle Paul's sternest and most impassioned letters—the New Testament epistle to the Galatians.

Galatian Legalism and Some-Grace Theology

Paul said he was astonished that those Galatian Christians were deserting Christ and his grace (see Gal. 1:6), and he put his finger on their some-grace error. Galatian believers began their faith lives relying totally on grace; later some fell away from grace (5:4) as the sole basis of being rightly related to God. Paul added explicitly that he, in contrast, had not set aside grace and replaced it with law-keeping as his source of righteousness (2:21). He implied that if believers can be right with God through their own law-keeping efforts, then Jesus' death on the cross was a colossal error of cosmic proportions.

Some-grace theology implies that we begin our Christian lives depending 100 percent upon Christ's righteousness, but over time that dependence decreases as we develop more righteousness of our own through our increasingly perfect law-keeping. We switch from grace to, as Dave used to say, "beavering for the Lord." Obviously the church depicted in the cartoon believed in beavering for the Lord.

"God may have already accepted you, but *our* standards are just a little higher."

Now, some-grace theology is closer to the truth than no-grace theology, but it still misses God's all-grace plan.

Biblical Truth: All-Grace Theology

Scripture declares that, as a contemporary hymn says, "Only by grace do we enter. Only by grace do we stand." We'll know we're entering and standing by grace alone when this following formula summarizes our beliefs:

JESUS + NOTHING ELSE = ACCEPTANCE BY GOD

Our salvation and right standing with God rests on Jesus' perfect performance, not ours. If it were the other way around, whose praises would we be singing throughout eternity? Why would we glorify and praise God the Father, God the Son, and God the Holy Spirit if we were the ones who did most of the work? You'd expect all Christians to warmly embrace an all-grace position, but they don't.

Churches and Grace

Some churches seem to fear that if the truth ever gets out about grace—God's gift of eternal life through Christ apart from any of our beavering—we'd all abandon biblical guidelines for conduct and become a pack of howling hedonists. This view misses the truth that genuinely grace-awed believers want to obey and please God. We love him as a natural response to his first loving us, not because we're trying to earn his favor.

Like the hurting and hurtful families they resemble, some-grace churches have expectations for their members that distort and deny the truth. In hurtful families, for example, expectations for children don't match the truth about child development and human imperfection. In the same way, some-grace churches' expectations of members don't match the biblical truth of spiritual growth and human imperfection. As a result problem-laden believers often feel different and worth less than the mythical perfect Christians they're told they should be. This leads to perfectionistic performing to earn the right to be with and relate to God and other supposedly perfect Christians. No wonder some-grace churches feel like stained glass-enclosed family reunions. No wonder the term "church home" brings chills, not thrills, to wounded worshipers.

Church, as God intended it to be, is the place where, when we sinners go there, other sinners have to take us in—and none of us have to deserve it! That's what a genuinely Bible-believing church will be. Yet, many of the some-grace churches who loudly proclaim themselves "Bible believing" beat the Galatians hands down with their legalism. If these churches were corporations, they could be reported to the

Better Business Bureau for misrepresentation and fraud—if for nothing else than how they distort the truth about God.

The Some-Grace Church's God

Some-grace churches frequently picture God as a combination frowning Pharisee and stern shepherd. This god angrily drives his sheep to jump through higher and higher spiritual hoops in hopes of winning his hard-earned acceptance. But no matter how hard we work, we can never run quite fast enough or jump quite high enough to fully satisfy this god. And what happens when we falter and fail? Well, let's just say it's not a pretty picture. He'll zap us with financial disasters and physical diseases to underscore his intolerance of our human imperfection and spiritual shortcomings.

Hurting people can fall for this kind of spiritual counterfeit if they don't have the genuine article through a personal relationship with Jesus. That means trusting God, which we aren't likely to do when we don't really know him.

Knowing the God of All-Grace

Most break*throughs* require a break *with*. This truth is well known to wounded worshipers who long to see God more accurately. As Roberta, an incest survivor, put it, "I had to let go of my father's god before God could become my Father." That's no easy task for an incest survivor, or for any wounded worshiper for that matter. Roberta and all of us need some way to learn what our Heavenly Father is truly like.

Knowing God: Provisions and Problems

The Bible provides the clearest picture of who God really is. But the Bible also presents a problem to wounded worshipers who have "Bible-phobia." In abusive churches, leaders often use Scripture as a weapon to keep members in line. So it's not surprising that for Bible-beaten folks Scripture feels like an instrument of torture.

Think of it this way. If as kids we were punched in the nose every time we opened the refrigerator, we stayed away from it and learned to survive on non-refrigerated food. Although creation reveals God's existence in a general way, we have no source of specific revelation about God except the Bible.

Bible phobia is not the same as failing to schedule time for God's Word. But when we can't read Scripture without losing concentration or feeling ill, we may need help to work through our spiritual abuse. God wants us to know him as he is revealed in Scripture, so we will trust and love him. God knows that an intimate love relationship with him is the source of our highest joy.

Trusting God: The Problems and the Purpose

God longs for us to know him. He put on skin so we could actually see his character and hear his heart. Jesus is that "God with us."

The night before Jesus died, one of his disciples asked to be shown the Father. (See John 14:8–9.) Healing for distorted God-concepts still flows from Jesus' awesome answer: "Anyone who has seen me has seen the Father." So when we wonder how God would relate to us in various life circumstances, we can find out by learning from Scripture how Jesus did it.

Jesus is not simply a discerning, departed teacher whose wise words are worth remembering. Jesus is, in fact, the invisible, living, perfect God-man who knows and loves us and calls us to know him spiritually and personally, so we will trust him. The thought of trusting anyone can be terrifying for hurting people. For some of us, that terror holds for God, too.

Disappointed with a "Broken Jesus"

When my husband and I went to see our week-old firstborn grandchild, we took several gifts, including a beautiful bisque music box that played "Jesus Loves Me" while the cradle holding baby Jesus (in the nativity scene on top) rocked. But when our son and daughter-in-law played it, they discovered a broken Jesus. He didn't do what he was supposed to do—rock. They decided to keep the music box anyway, and we all still refer to it as "Broken Jesus."

Many wounded worshipers have a broken Jesus, too. He isn't working the way we were told he would. We thought our Christian lives were supposed to be consistently easy and constantly exciting. We hoped soon to be healthy, wealthy, wise, and hassle-free! (I know I did.)

But these unrealistic, unbiblical expectations about the Christian life are not the only problems we face when it comes to trusting God. Many of us can't seem to make it past our pain.

The Pain Barrier

It's nearly impossible for Christians who grew up in substantially healthy homes to fathom the depth of distrust abuse survivors feel. God is so much more realistic about all this than we are. For example, in Exodus 6:9 the Hebrews in Egyptian bondage couldn't really hear Moses' message from God because of their "anguish of spirit and cruel bondage." And it was a pretty impressive message: God had chosen them to be his people; he would be their God in a special relationship which included their release from bondage.

We need to understand verses like this as God's giving us permission to be as honest about the influence of authentic emotions in our lives as he is, even when those emotions include unspeakable terror that blocks our ability to trust.

Our families and friends may not give us permission to be fully human, feelings and all, but God does! This wonderful sketch found on the next page may help you as much as it helps me when I need to remember this truth.

God isn't horrified when out of our pain and despair we cry, "Why didn't you stop it? Why do you let it continue? Don't you care? What kind of Father are you?"

God wants us to bring our honest fears, questions, and anguish to him so we can experience his comforting embrace. He loves us and understands far better than we that until we know that, we won't relate to him with trusting love.

Loving and Relating to God

Oh, that we could get it straight once and for all. *God loves us because of who he is, not because of who we are!*

"SURELY HE HATH BORNE OUR GRIEFS, AND CARRIED OUR SORROWS..." ISA 53:4

This all-grace good news of God's love and acceptance sounds too good to be true to many of us. Especially to those of us weaned on the teaching "anything worth having is worth working for!" That must-work-for-it attitude sounds so logical. Yet, the more I learn about God, the more I think he loves standing our best logic right on its head.

The relationship rules we learned in hurting families, the pathetic impersonations of perfection designed to guarantee acceptance, all melt away in the warmth of God's unreasonable grace. Still, it is hard for many of us to lay aside all our fancy footwork on the religious straight and narrow. What joy in heaven there must be when we finally collapse under the weight of our shame-fueled, fear-driven no-grace or some-grace religiosity! Only then can we experience God's love for us—for the *real* you and the *real* me.

Jesus Loves (the Real) Me, This I (Finally) Know

My worst enemies could not be more surprised than I am at God's awesome, gracious love poured out on me, because I know more awful things about me than they do. And God knows far more than either they or I ever will. And you know the really amazing part? God loves me anyway!

As a Christian since age thirteen, I knew God loved me because the Bible told me so several decades before I knew it in a deeply personal way. There is a world of difference between knowing *about* God's love theologically, and know-ing God's love *experientially*. That difference forever changed my relationship with God. It will do the same for you.

Specific Change Strategies

Some of you may sense the need for a little help and healing before you more deeply and personally experience God's life-changing love. As always, we ground our change process in truth.

1. *Begin thinking of God as Jesus.* If you are really serious about healing your spiritual abuse wounds, make an intentional choice to begin picturing Jesus whenever you think or talk about God. Don't you think it's time to stop, in effect, calling God by your father's, grandfather's, uncle's, or someone else's name, and start calling him Jesus?

   Read and study the Gospels to learn how Jesus inter-acted with people. How did he treat people who were struggling with sin? Jesus was astonishingly kind and gentle with the people who knew they were sinful, and amazingly confrontive with those who thought they were perfect.

2.   *Learn about God's general attributes.* Learning to see God as he is revealed in Scripture, most clearly in Jesus, will help replace distorted God-concepts with the truth. This will help you love and trust God more. (To help you get started, Appendix E lists some of God's attributes.)

3.   *Learn about how God is a loving parent.* God wants us to know that he is not like hurtful human parents. In Psalm 27:10 he says that though our own parents forsake us, he will "receive" us (NIV) or "take care of" us (NKJV). This verse seems to picture God reaching down to adopt us as his own children, the way a loving human father would "receive" a child abandoned on his doorstep. Scripture repeatedly emphasizes God's tender concern for "the fatherless" and for orphans. See Psalms 10:14 and 146:9 and Hosea 14:3. As a fatherless child, those verses are especially precious to me.

4.   *Write about what you're learning.* Use your personal journal to write about how God differs from your parent-shaped perceptions of him and how that truth could change your life if you began acting on it. This is an example written by a Christian adult raised by hurtful, perfectionistic parents.

> I am blown away by Jesus' description of the father in the Prodigal Son parable. He is entirely different from my dad. I have been afraid and very reluctant to confess my sins to God because I always pictured Him with His arms folded over His chest, shaking His head back and forth, with a disgusted look on His face—just like my dad. I think I can pray more easily if I can hold on to the picture of God as loving and forgiving.

5.   *Get help to deal honestly with the pain of the pain.* As we begin to honestly mourn our childhood losses and feel the grief and despair, the pain can be nearly debilitating. The worst part may be the pain of the pain. That's what a Christian survivor of childhood abuse in a satanic cult family calls the pain of realizing that God allowed her to

be abused—no, *tortured* is a better description—in ways that can only be called supernaturally evil.

I would not insult this or other refugees from childhood hells by offering an easy answer to the imponderable questions such experiences raise. I don't know why our loving Father God permits little children to undergo such unspeakable suffering. But I cling to my belief that somehow, in some way, light-years beyond my capacity to understand, God will fulfill his promises to comfort the mourning and bring joy out of our pain. (See Isa. 61:2–3 and Ps. 30:11.)

The pain of our pain is that God allowed it. I think the joy of our joy must be learning that God really can heal and redeem our pain and lead us into lives of genuine joy.

6. *Choose to trust God in the midst of your pain and questions.* If we wait, until we stop doubting and hurting before we trust God, we'll never do it. God never promises his children pain-free lives in this sin-stained world. He does promise to be with us and to comfort and strengthen us in the midst of our pain. I invite you to purposefully decide to trust God after examining his record of faithfulness to that promise. If you are willing to practice this choice (or even willing to be made willing), ask God to empower you.

7. *Choose your church family.* We couldn't choose our birth families, but now we can choose our church families. Deliberately evaluate your church's spiritual health and decide if you should stay. See Appendix F for a practical comparison of shame-based and grace-based churches. Look for a church that has the biblically balanced emphasis of 2 Peter 3:18, which instructs believers to "grow in the grace and knowledge of our Lord and Savior Jesus Christ." Ask God to lead you in this critical choice.

Worshipers' H.O.P.E. Chart

KEY ISSUES	SEEING TRUTH	NEW CHOICES	NEW PRACTICING
Learning to Separate God's Traits from Our Parents' Traits	I've been relating to God as if he had the same expectations as my parents	Learn more about God's true character by learning more about Jesus	Relate consistently to God on the basis of his attributes as revealed in Jesus
Living by All-grace Theology	Sometimes I live as if I don't need any grace or only some at the start of my faith life	Study the Bible to discover the role of God's grace in being rightly related to God	Relate consistently to God on an all-grace basis of trust in Jesus' righteousness and death for my sins
Choosing to Trust God for Comfort	I've trusted God to keep me pain-free or not trusted him to comfort and guide	Learn from Scripture how faithful and trustworthy God has proven to be	Consistently choose to trust God for comfort in my pain and for guidance in my life

---

Pause to Ponder and Pray

PONDER: Use the H.O.P.E. chart to find where you are in your changing and healing process in the area of spiritual wounds.

✔ What surprised you most about God as you read Appendix E?

✔ Review the characteristics of some-grace theology churches and all-grace theology churches in Appendix F. Which does your current church resemble more?

PRAY: Lord, please help me see you as the loving Father your Word and your Son show you to be. Please teach me to trust you in the midst of my doubts and pain. Thanks for understanding how difficult all of this is for me. Amen.

Just Ahead

Many of God's attributes are, as theologians say, non-communicable. This means that only God, not human beings, has, for example, unlimited power. However, God elects to share some of his attributes, including that of forgiving. And this means that human beings have the capacity to be forgiving, too.

Some of us aren't entirely convinced about that. More on the scary topic of forgiveness next.

CHAPTER
Thirteen

Help for Healing Forgivers

How can God bear knowing all the details of all the hurts of all the ages?

I can hardly stand knowing a fraction of the facts about one clergyman who molested nearly a hundred boys and girls for years, while his superiors moved him from one parish to another when his crimes threatened to become widely known. Scores of men and women have testified publicly of their abuse at his hands. Yet, incomprehensibly, in spite of an earlier confession, he denied his guilt.

I'm torn between weeping and raging over just this one hideous, hurtful example of human treachery and betrayal of trust. What of those so unblinkingly betrayed? What of their parents who also trusted the betrayers? What of the bitter agony when we are the children or the parents thus betrayed? What can we do? Where do we go? How can we bear such life-shattering injustice and pain?

Baring the Unbearable

When I can't bear it, whatever "it" may be, my best choice is to bare it to the Lord. Bare it as in uncovering rather than hiding it. Bear it also in the sense of carrying it somewhere. I picture myself bearing on a large platter the situation that's too heavy for me to carry and too painful for me to bear. Then I lay the platter I've borne at the nail-scarred feet of Jesus.

In this chapter, we'll learn that the imaginary scene I've just described is a picture of forgiveness. We'll face the need to forgive ourselves, as well as those who have hurt us deeply. Usually when we've been raised in hurtful families, this includes forgiving our parents. Before we work our way up to that though, let's try to untangle the thicket of truths and myths that make forgiving so difficult.

The Facts and Fallacies About Forgiving

Finding our way through the tangled underbrush of forgiveness facts and fallacies can be quite an adventure. You're probably not surprised to learn that our most trustworthy map is Scripture. One of my favorite guides is that Old Testament hero, Joseph.

We read about Joseph, the pampered rich man's son, in the last twenty-three chapters of Genesis. Years after his older brothers had sold him into Egyptian slavery, clever and godly Joseph was in a position second only to Pharaoh. When his brothers came to buy grain for their famine-stricken families, they didn't recognize Joseph. But he certainly knew them. Joseph had the perfect opportunity to get even!

Obviously, since Joseph is our forgiveness guide, he chose to pass up his chance. However, his brothers always believed that some way at some time Joseph would take revenge on them. So when their father died, they fell before Joseph, afraid he'd waited until then to get even.

The brothers' please-forgive-us-for-treating-you-so-badly-and-we'll-be-your-slaves speech brought Joseph's reply as recorded in Genesis 50:20. "You intended to harm me, but God intended it for good to accomplish what is now being done, the saving of many lives" (NIV). This verse focuses on the first of two major facts about forgiving.

Fact 1: Genuine Forgiving Is Founded on Ruthless Realism

Joseph didn't beat around the bush. He told his brothers he knew they had intentionally chosen to harm him. God never calls us to play around with truth or fake it for Jesus' sake. He never does that—not even in an area as important as forgiving.

One clear forgiveness truth features God as sole dispenser of judgment on those who wrong us. Genesis 50:19 reveals that Joseph told his brothers he would not usurp God's place by punishing them for their sins against him. That sounds just fine for Joseph and his brothers, but God's timetable doesn't always match our own, and that's not always so fine.

Do you ever wonder why God is so slow to execute judgment on evildoers? Second Peter 3:15 gives a clear answer. God patiently extends opportunities to evildoers to turn to him for salvation. So what we label *slowness* is actually God's gracious patience.

While Joseph did not take revenge or execute judgment on his wrongdoers, he did not excuse, minimize, or discount the wrong done to him. Many of us tend to deny the full extent of our hurters' wounding ways. We excuse, minimize, and discount the hurt as though whatever happened—no matter how horrendous—couldn't have been all that bad since we survived. That was Carol Jean's perspective.

"This sounds pretty bad, doesn't it, but really it's okay; it's not as bad as it sounds." I heard Carol Jean repeat that sentence scores of times when she first began to remember and talk about her neglect and abuse as a child. Minimizing her wounds served to protect her from experiencing the full load of pain attached to the truth of her self-absorbed parents' loveless parenting. With a child's typical magical thinking, Carol Jean had concluded that she caused her parents' behavior because she was, as she put it, "an unusually bad child." That perception created the sense of shame that made her folks' actions seem "not as bad as it sounds," because Carol Jean thought of herself as worth less than other people.

I've discovered one sure way of injecting a massive dose of realism into shame-bound adults' perceptions of their treatment as children. And I used this approach with Carol Jean. Since she was single and childless, I asked her to think of one of our pastor's little girls who was then the same age Carol Jean had been during the abusive experience she had just recalled and quickly minimized. Then I asked if what she just described would have been okay if it had happened to the pastor's daughter.

Carol Jean's face changed instantly. "Oh, dear God, no! Of course not. No!" she exclaimed in horror.

"Then what makes it okay for you?" I asked softly.

I ask you the same question as you face the hurts you need to forgive. Shame says that whatever treatment I get is okay because after all, *it's just me.*

Sometimes people think this attitude is appropriately humble and helpful to their changing processes. But denial of truth actually impedes the healing we long to experience. We must forgive our hurters to live in the freedom God intends for us. And to be genuinely effective, forgiving demands ruthless realism. That means we must name the deeds done to us, just as Joseph did, stop anesthetizing the emotions that accompany such deeds, and begin feeling those emotions.

Ruthless realism also includes recognizing that our hurters were once children, too, and that they were likely abandoned by neglect or terrorized by abuse. This reality in no way excuses their wrong choices about how to treat us. Understanding a behavior does not make it acceptable. We must be clear about this, because learning more about those who wounded us helps us forgive them without excusing or accepting their wrong choices.

Another ruthless reality confronts us with the fact that unforgiveness can feel like a powerful position in relationships. It's as if we say, "I'll show them! They withheld so much from me for so long, I'll withhold forgiveness." One of the fallacies of this rationale is that our parents or other hurters may never even notice or care that we've withheld forgiveness. In fact, refusing to forgive is a bit like having a toddler's temper tantrum. So even if our parents get alarmed that we're holding our breath, so to speak, we are the ones who turn blue and get dizzy.

The bottom line of ruthless realism that Joseph modeled is this: Genuine forgiveness forces us to relinquish our tightly clutched fantasies of pasts that never were, so that we can see what is and what can be.

If this whole forgiving process sounds like a pretty scary, messy business, you're right. But, take heart. Joseph's experience reveals the secret to surviving the pain of genuine forgiving.

Fact 2: Genuinely Forgiving Is for Those in God's Family

By faith as God's child, Joseph had access to his heavenly Father's provisions. We see that most clearly in Genesis 41:51-52, where Joseph credits God with enabling him to move beyond the pain of his past into a life of fruitfulness.

We will never find the motivation or means to fully forgive ourselves or others unless we respond to the moving of God in our hearts, as Joseph did. When we stop to think about it, forgiving is an unnatural, illogical act. This is a dog-eat-dog world, not a dog-*forgive*-dog world. On a personal level, we're more naturally inclined to collect eyes for eyes and teeth for teeth than to write off the wrongs done to us. It's little wonder we bump and bruise each other as we stagger blind and toothless through our lives.

Forgiving is family business. God wants his children to bear some likeness, however imperfect, to him, their Father. That's the message of verses such as Ephesians 4:32 that tell us to be kind and forgiving as our Father God is. But neither God's promises nor commands are intended for universal application. You may be trying to live by the Father's rules when you aren't even the Father's child. You need to begin forgiving by receiving forgiveness.

Receiving Forgiveness and Forgiving Ourselves

This is my fourth book with a chapter on forgiveness. In the others, I wrote about forgiving ourselves after I first discussed forgiving others. Since I believe it's often more difficult to forgive ourselves, I was trying to sneak up on that gigantic task.

I'm reversing the order this time to emphasize that unless we truly understand and personally experience forgiveness, it is impossible to forgive others. Especially when those others are parents who betrayed the tender trust of our childhoods. The biblical basis for this "me first" order in forgiving is in Matthew's gospel, chapter 18. Jesus told a story in answer to Peter's question about how much forgiving God expects from his children (see verses 23-35).

A king confronts one of his servants about repaying a multimillion-dollar debt. The servant asks the king to be patient and promises to repay everything. However, the king takes pity on the servant, releases him, and cancels the debt.

After the now debt-free servant leaves, he finds another servant who owes him a few dollars and demands immediate payment. The second servant also asks for patience and promises to repay everything as well. But the first servant refuses and has the poor man thrown into prison. When the king hears about this, he summons the first servant, denounces his lack of mercy, and turns him over to "the torturers until he should pay all that was due." What can we learn from the points in this story about the relationship between having our unpayable debts canceled and canceling the debts of others? We can learn at least five principles.

1. *Point*: The first servant underestimated his debt and overestimated his ability to repay. That's why he asked for patience rather than mercy.

    Principle: We all underestimate the enormity of our sin debt and overestimate our own ability to do enough good deeds to balance the scales.

2. *Point*: The king understood the truth about the debt and the servant-debtor, so he gave the mercy that was needed, instead of the time that was requested.

    Principle: God understands the depths of our sin and our spiritual bankruptcy, even though we don't. Therefore, while we keep asking what we can do to earn eternal life, God continues to tell us in Scripture that he canceled

our sin-debt with Jesus' death on the cross. (See Col.
2:13–14.)

3. *Point*: The debt-free servant did not really hear the
king's incredibly gracious words, so he believed he still
owed a debt he needed to pay eventually.
Principle: This seems to capture the essence of some-
grace theology we examined in the last chapter. The
servant asked for some grace, in effect, in the form of
patience, but figured he could do the rest on his own.

4. *Point*: That's why the first servant sought to collect a
relatively small debt which his fellow servant actually
might have been able to repay in time.
Principle: Operating from a some-grace perspective
means we don't have enough grace-consciousness to
extend grace to those who sin against us.

5. *Point*: The servant who refused to cancel a debt because
he didn't believe his own debt was canceled, missed out
on the joy of living debt-free, and experienced imprison-
ment and torture instead.
Principle: People who see themselves as unreleased and
debt-laden won't release others and cancel their debts.
As a result, the unreleasing debt collectors live in tortur-
ous bondage.

Good News and Bad News About Forgiveness

Our worst and God's best met on a battlefield called Calvary. God won! Jesus' spread-eagled victory there is God's
Good News grace-gift to us if we'll receive it.

I recently read an amazing story from the past century
about a man sentenced to death for robbing a stagecoach. For
many reasons, President Andrew Jackson pardoned him.
But, to everyone's dismay, the condemned man refused the
pardon. His case finally reached the Supreme Court. This is
a portion of the Court's opinion:

> A pardon is an act of grace. . . . A pardon is a deed, to the
> validity of which delivery is essential, and delivery is not
> complete without acceptance.[1]

Like this robber and the first servant in Jesus' story, we've been pardoned—released from our unpayable sin-debt. (Essentially, forgiveness means pardon or release from a debt.[2]) But like the pardoned man and the debt-free servant, we must accept the gift given us and stop striving to pay our sky-high debts ourselves.

Curiously, many Christians who've actually received God's gift of forgiveness still struggle with forgiving themselves. I know. I was one of them for years. I've met other Christians who've also used self-punishing guilt in an attempt to make themselves behave better. The logic seems to be something like: I hate myself for what I did, because I hurt myself and others horribly. I will trust my ongoing guilt-driven self-punishment to keep me from sinning that way again.

Believe me, this is bad news! That reasoning keeps us so focused on what we have done, we virtually ignore what Christ has done for us. Without a shift of focus from our sins to God's grace, we'll never experience the freedom forgiveness brings. And only the forgiven can truly forgive.

Forgiving Our Parents

"It isn't just what they did. It's who did it!" That's how George described what hurt him most about growing up with a verbally abusive mother and a physically abusive father.

Parents are supposed to lovingly nurture and protect their children, but as we know so well, they don't always do that. If we come from hurtful families, we usually have more to forgive than mere *childhood* wounds. To rephrase a greeting card company's slogan, we might say a hurtful parent's wounding is "the gift that goes on giving."

I've told you enough about my mother-focused childhood for you to guess that I remained overly invested emotionally in my mother's life well into my adult years. So you can imagine how shocked I was when Mother phoned me many years ago to matter-of-factly announce that she'd been married for six weeks to a man I'd never even heard her mention. Of course, I maintained my cheery, "sunshine" voice throughout our conversation. In fact it was weeks before I let myself feel the tangled mix of emotions that call triggered.

I felt so abandoned and betrayed. I remember repeating to myself, "I would never have done that to her!" And it was true. I also began to feel an indescribable sense of having been suckered by Mother into working hard, jumping through hoops, and twisting myself into a human pretzel my entire life trying to make her happy because she counted on me so much. And just how important was I to her after all? She didn't bother telling me about her wedding until six weeks after the fact, let alone invite me to attend or participate. It was her *wedding*, for heaven's sake! That was one of my earliest clues to just how deeply wounded and self-absorbed my mother was.

I realize that experience pales in comparison to many of your examples of how wounding parents continue their hurtful ways in our adult lives. Unless our hurtful parents, and the other significant hurters in our lives, open themselves to the healing touch of God, they are apt to go on wounding us to some degree as long as they or we live.

We need to do something with the growing mountains of hurt that threaten to crush us with hatred and bitterness. Releasing the hurts and the hurters is our only hope. And if we can release our parents, the rest of the wounding world is a cinch.

Releasing Our Hurtful Parents

What we hold, holds us. This is true of our belief systems as well as our inability to forgive. This slogan is a kind of Monkey Trap Model for understanding the releasing function of forgiveness.

Pause a moment and look at one of your hands. (You can hold the book in the other.) Now pick up something small and unbreakable with your free hand and hold the object tightly. You have to make a fist of your hand to do that, don't you? Here's where the Monkey Trap reference applies.

A monkey is trapped when he slips his hand into a tiny opening in a small wire cage containing something he desires, such as a banana. The monkey grasps the object in his fist and tries to pull his hand through the trap's tiny opening. Of course, the balled-up, banana-clutching fist is too large to get through. The monkey is trapped unless he releases what's in his hand. Apparently monkeys usually are unwilling to let go.

Now, turn your hand palm down and open it, and notice what happens. As you release what you are holding, it in effect releases you. Now your hand is free to reach for anything you want.

Unfair or Unhealthy?

"But it seems so unfair for me to be hurt again and again without somebody admitting it or paying for it," you may say in response to the idea of releasing your hurters. You might even think you could forgive and release if the wounding ones just said they were sorry. But even if they did, I doubt that their level of repentance would match their level of wounding. Likely you wouldn't feel satisfied.

I recently watched a T.V. special on child abuse. The host talked with a convicted incest perpetrator and one of the two stepdaughters he had abused sexually for nearly a decade. Although he had served nine years in prison for his crime, he was reluctant to own his sin against his stepdaughters. Even when he finally did, his admission was half-hearted, voiced only after the host repeatedly confronted the man's failure to accept full responsibility. That level of "well-if-I-hurt-you-I'm-sorry" kind of pseudo-repentance fell far short of his level of wounding.

Surely a wound-matching level of repentance would likely make forgiving easier. But would that actually pay for deep wounds caused by repeated betrayals of trust? What could our hurters possibly do today to make up for what they did yesterday? In effect, they owe us debts they can never repay.

Our hurters stand before us with empty hands and pockets, utterly unable to pay for the past. And we stand facing the choices that will shape our futures. We can keep trying to collect debts rightfully owed us by exacting verbal and nonverbal tolls. But that means constantly replaying the painful past to keep our hurters' deficits fresh on our mental balance sheets. Or we can cancel their debts and forgive them. Remember, forgiving is not denying the wounders' wrongs. Forgiving means we release the right to wrong them in return.

Does that mean they got away with it? Not really. I seriously doubt that anyone ever really gets away with sin. But that's not what our acts of forgiving mean anyway. Forgiving means we choose to release the sins and the sinners into the nail-scarred hands of the only One qualified to judge. It also means that we are released from our bondage to bitterness.

Jesus, the Truth, is also the Way out of our bitterness traps. The self-wounding fantasies we've harbored say, "I'll be better off holding on to this bitterness and hatred." If that's such an effective self-protection strategy, then why are we in so much pain?

Maybe unforgiveness by refusing to release our debtors can hurt us more than it hurts them. Consider what a physician, Arnold Fox, has concluded about refusing to forgive:

> Forgiveness allows your body to turn down the manufacture of those chemicals which are tearing you apart, body and soul. Doctors can give you all sorts of medicines for your headaches, your heart, your stomach pains, your spastic colon, your anxiety, and other problems. But the medicines will not get to the root of the problem: Unforgiveness. The cure for that lies in forgiving. When you savor your hatred, you don't hurt *them*, you hurt yourself.[3]

Resentment and bitterness actually are malevolent forms of intense interpersonal attachment, like being tied to our hurters with barbed wire. Staying impaled on that barbed wire of bitterness means we continue to miss the truth that we are the ones most bloodied, not they. As this poem says, we need to release the prisoner.

Release the Prisoner

"Release the prisoner!
Release or he will die."

Release the prisoner?
"Where's justice?" my reply.

"Release the prisoner!"
I heard again the cry.

Release the prisoner?
At last I said I'd try.

Release the prisoner—
With Grace my sole supply,

I released the prisoner
and saw that it was I.[4]

Releasing our hurtful parents and others includes recognizing the ruthless reality that they are as bankrupt before us as we are before God. Thus forgiving and releasing means handing our hurters' unpayable sin debts to God to settle. Isn't that what we had to do with our own?

Keeping score of others' wrongs takes enormous emotional energy. If we finally snip our barbed-wire bitterness and release them, we might be ready to move on to consider an even more outrageous proposal.

Choosing Our Parents

Choose my parents? You've got to be kidding! That was my response when I heard a wise people-helper say we must all someday come to the point of choosing our parents. In so doing we choose God and we choose ourselves. I knew I had heard something as profound as it was unsettling, but I wasn't ready to wrestle with it just then. So I locked it tightly in my emotion-proof cognitive box until later.

In a few days (I was thinking in terms of months or years) God's Holy Spirit shattered my intellectualization during a time of Bible study and prayer. In my minds eye I began to see a long line of smiling young mothers walking past a hospital nursery window looking in at me as I looked up at them from my bassinet. When I saw my own mother, as she appears in the one photograph I have of her with me as a baby, I reached up and sensed myself being lifted into her waiting arms. I could feel my tiny, infant body enfolded by her arms and resting on her shoulder.

I sobbed and sobbed, clutching a sofa pillow to my chest and abdomen as if to keep my emotional guts from exploding through my skin. Between sobs, I began to repeat aloud, "Yes, Mother, I choose you because God chose you for me." (Tears come to my eyes now as I write this.) I also "told" my mother that I remembered many painful circumstances, but I was still choosing her. I thanked her for loving me, for fighting to give me life, and especially, for teaching me about God's love.

I was completely exhausted when I finished and felt as if I'd lost about fifty pounds from right over my heart. While I have very meaningful and precious times of prayer and Bible study on a regular basis, that sort of experience is definitely not business-as-usual!

Many of you, no doubt, are appalled by the thought of choosing your parents, just as I was. At least consider the idea that until we emotionally accept, receive, and yes, *choose* our parents, we are rejecting the instruments of our births and our genetic endowments. This symbolic, emotional choice in no way negates the reality of our parents' behavior toward us, for God never asks us to deny pain and terrible truth. God asks us to choose to trust him to heal the pain and transform the truth.

Forgiveness, Boundaries, and Reconciliation

Maybe we recoil at the notion of choosing our parents because we believe that means we'd forfeit the right to establish any personal boundaries with them. In reality, neither releasing our parents to God nor receiving our parents from God requires relinquishing healthy interpersonal boundaries. Why? Because grace is free; trust is earned.

This crucial distinction means we can forgive our folks or others for their sins against us but it doesn't mean we are going to give them unlimited access to our lives. Boundaries mark levels of trust. If you embezzle funds from my company, I can forgive you but I don't need to ask you to be my accountant.

But what about reconciliation? Don't we have to fully reconcile when we fully forgive? I don't think so. If we're using the plumb line of Scripture to determine our actions and reactions, we'll see that reconciliation is rooted in both parties' agreeing about the truth of the wrongdoing in question. (See 2 Cor. 5:18–21.) The forgiven but unforgiving servant in our story was never really reconciled to the king, despite that gracious monarch's debt-cancellation, because he never agreed with the king's assessment of his debt.

Similarly, when deeply wounded folks extend forgiveness and seek reconciliation, many experience rejection and revictimization by their abusers. Their hurters may call them "crazy," "liars," or worse, none of which agree with the truth about the wounding.

Some counselors say that we can never truly forgive without confronting. This well-meaning advice is like the idea that we must fully reconcile to fully forgive. What if our hurters are dead? We can neither reconcile nor confront them. Even when they are alive, they can short-circuit a reconciliation with lies, and we may prayerfully conclude that confrontation about hands-off hurts isn't wise.

If we do choose the confrontation route, we will need some practical, prayer-filled preparation. That holds for every step in this excruciating, crucial journey called forgiveness.

There are two overarching reasons why God talks so much about forgiving. First, we only have other sinners with whom to relate, so God knows we'll need to become skillful forgivers. Second, I think God structures our healing and changing processes so they require us to forgive, because the alternative is so much worse.

Specific Change Strategies

1. *Receive God's forgiveness and forgive yourself.* Remember, people who feel unforgiven are poor forgivers. Using the prayer at the end of Chapter 7, or similar words, you

can commit yourself to God and receive his forgiveness through Christ. Then you can begin focusing on God's grace instead of your sins.

2. *Adopt and structure an "event-and-process" perspective on forgiving.* The best analogy I know to illustrate this experience comes from the years my husband and I lived on a tiny lake. Sailing from our dock to the lake's end began with an event that included a decision to reach that goal. It also required a process of continually recommitting to that goal as gusts of wind and our own wandering attention got us off course.

Write a forgiveness statement to mark your formal forgiving event. This statement can help you head back toward your forgiveness goal when gusts of new memories arise and emotional storms blow you temporarily off course.

Sharing your decision to forgive with a friend or counselor reinforces the reality of your choice.

3. *Relabel those you've forgiven.* This is especially meaningful when forgiving parents. For example, you might relabel by changing "she is the *guilty mother*" to "she is the *mother released to God.*"

4. *Get help to process the often intense and painful emotions that accompany forgiveness work.* My admittedly simple forgiveness formula is: Face it, feel it, and forgive it. That second step can be a killer. Don't try to do a Lone Ranger imitation in this changing, healing journey we've undertaken, especially when it comes to working through the pain of forgiving.

Forgivers' H.O.P.E. Chart

KEY ISSUES	SEEING TRUTH	NEW CHOICES	NEW PRACTICING
Understanding what genuine forgiveness is and is not	I don't understand what genuine, biblical forgiving is	Learn about what genuine forgiving is and is not	Consistently practice genuinely biblical forgiving
Experiencing the Reality of God's Forgiveness	I have not accepted the gift of God's forgiveness in Christ	Ask for and receive God's forgiveness by accepting Christ's payment for my sin debt	Living more often in the freedom and joy of knowing my entire sin debt is paid
Releasing My Hurters into God's Hands	I have refused to forgive and release those who've hurt me	Consider the benefits of forgiving and releasing those who've hurt me	Actually forgive and emotionally release my hurters to God

Pause to Ponder and Pray

PONDER: Use the H.O.P.E. chart to find where you are in your changing and healing process of forgiveness.

✔ Were you surprised by what forgiveness is and is not?

✔ Where are you in the three-step forgiveness formula of face the hurt, feel it, and forgive it?

✔ If you're stuck, unable to move to the next step in the formula, will you get some help?

If so, when?

PRAY: Lord, thank you for paying my sin debt since I never could. Please empower and comfort me as I face the truth and feel the pain of my hurts, so that I can forgive others as you've forgiven me. Amen.

Just Ahead

I'm sure you noticed that I focused on our parents as the "others" we'll likely struggle most with forgiving, because they had such emotional power in our childhoods. Perhaps they still do. When we honestly acknowledge the emotional power our parents wield in our lives, we are confronted with the uncomfortable reality that we have enormous influence in our children's lives. In the next chapter, we'll see how we can harness that influence for helping instead of hurting.

CHAPTER
Fourteen

Help for Healing Parents

Anything that begins with the word *labor* can't be easy! Clearly this is true when it comes to parenting.

Many of us parents who grew up in hurtful homes use the Muddle-Through Model of parenting with our own children. We feel like we're trying to perform brain surgery in a dark room at midnight with one hand tied behind us while we are blindfolded. We suspect there's a lot we need to know that we don't know. Worse yet, we don't know what we don't know!

In this chapter, we'll examine the effects of and remedies for that knowledge deficit. As we do, we'll focus on a few special parenting challenges we face when we come from significantly unhealthy families. Our goal will be learning how to give our children much of what we never received from our own parents. Brain surgery is child's play compared to a task like that.

The Shame School for Hurtful Parenting

Scratch most of us parents and we hemorrhage guilt and shame. As a member of an Adult Children of Dysfunctional Families support group put it, "My greatest fear is that twenty or thirty years from now, *my* kids will be coming to this group!" We know personally how powerful parents' influences can be on their children, as the cartoon depicts.

"ISN'T THAT CUTE? RALPH'S FOLLOWING
IN HIS FATHER'S FOOTSTEPS."

We actually might have more influence than we want to have with our children! I think of this when I hear parents say, "But I didn't mean to hurt my kids." I honestly believe that's true in the vast majority of situations involving hurtful parents.

Most parents do the best they know, but rarely do they do the best they could. And what traps them and us into repeating painful parenting patterns is our unwillingness to acknowledge that we are imperfect and our knowledge is faulty. Once again we see the hurtful legacy of shame.

Imagine the world of interpersonal relationships as a ballroom. I am there and I have two broken legs. Because I believe that broken legs are unforgivable moral flaws, I won't acknowledge my leg problem. I insist on dancing every number, no matter the tempo, while pretending my legs are fine. What's more, I refuse all offers of assistance while I stumble here, stagger there, and generally leave a trail of crushed toes, bruised ankles, and broken legs in my zigzagging wake.

That admittedly strange scene pictures our parenting patterns if we still operate from a shame-shaped mindset that says problems are unforgivable moral flaws. Since, to some degree, all of us are hurt people, in effect, we all have broken legs. The more shame-bound we are, the more we'll deny that reality and refuse life-changing assistance.

Who is most likely to get clobbered in our zigzagging wakes? Those closest to us, including our children. Then, to continue our analogy, *their* legs are bruised, so that our children develop self-protective, problematic perfect-leg pretenses of their own. If they, too, operate from a shame-based mindset, in time our grandchildren will join this painful intergenerational dance.

Now imagine our hypothetical ballroom is very dimly lit. Slowly the lights come up and we begin to recognize the extent of our wounding ways on those nearest and dearest to us, including our children. From one corner of the ballroom to the other, voices begin wailing, "But I didn't mean to crush your toes, bruise your ankles, or break your legs. I danced the best I could!"

That's where we are when, as parents, we recognize the extent of our wounds and our wounding ways. Some of us are so overwhelmed, we begin to focus all our attention on our children, whatever their ages, because we want them to experience healing and mending in their bruised and broken places. In our concern for our children, we often lose sight of a truth we hear proclaimed each time we board a commercial plane.

Secure Your Own Oxygen Mask First

Once when I actually listened to a flight attendant's safety speech, I heard a parable that captures a major struggle for parents raised in unhealthy homes. After covering the emergency exits and flotation cushions stuff, the flight attendant said something like, "In case of a problem with the cabin pressure, oxygen masks will automatically be released. If you are traveling with small children, secure your own oxygen mask first; then secure your child's mask."

I believe the attendant's instructions about oxygen masks convey an indispensable parenting truth: Unless we first help ourselves by choosing life-giving truth and change, we won't be able to help our children do the same. This me-first approach can feel inexcusably selfish to us, especially when we are genuinely concerned for our children. (In fact I questioned the wisdom of the flight attendant's oxygen-mask instructions the first time I heard them. Didn't you?)

It's as if, clutching our throats and nearly unconscious, we gasp, "I can't be bothered worrying about my breathing. Just tell me how to help my children breathe better." That is when we must remember the flight attendant's message: If we don't first reach for help for ourselves, we will not be able to help our children no matter how much we love them. I know the truth of this principle all too well.

Over twenty years ago, when my children were seven and nine, I parented from the Twilight Zone for about six months. Clinical depression turned me into a virtual zombie. I lived the Job 14:21–22 description of a parent's personal pain blocking awareness of her children's ups and downs.

Things got so bad that our family physician referred me to a psychiatrist. With a depressive's characteristic self-loathing, I considered neither I nor my emotional condition important enough to warrant paying a psychiatrist's fee. I truly believed that, despite the fact that I was sleeping about eighteen hours most days and my doctor said I was irreparably damaging my body.

I finally went to a psychiatrist, took medication I despised, and began the painful process of healing unseen wounds. I did it for only one reason: I did not want to continue sleeping away Becky's and Dave's childhoods. Depression depleted my capacity to care about myself and nearly everything else in life, but it didn't destroy my love for my children. But loving my children wasn't enough to help either them or me. I loved them even as I slept away their lives and mine. I had to let that love motivate me to reach for my own oxygen mask, so to speak. My desire to be a healthier parent forced me to become a healthier person!

One of the most challenging aspects of that process involved separating lies from the truth.

Major Challenge 1: Separating Parenting Lies from Truths

You'll spot the mixture of shame and magical thinking in the parenting lies listed in the following chart.[1]

Comparing Parenting Lies and Truths

LIE	TRUTH
1. Parents are giant geniuses who will *always* be smarter and stronger than their children.	1. Parents are older human beings, so they have more information and physical strength than children. Under normal circumstances, children will be about as smart (or smarter) and as strong (or stronger) *someday*.
2. Children are selfish and cause trouble when they have personal needs of their own that inconvenience their parents.	2. All children have legitimate personal needs that often inconvenience their parents. This is one of the realities of parenting.
3. All parents are supposed to protect and direct their children *forever* since parents will *always* know more than their children.	3. Parents are supposed to protect and direct their children while they are young. As children get older, parents are supposed to teach them how to protect themselves in most situations, and how to seek God's protection and direction in all situations.
4. Parents are supposed to love their children more when they obey them and make them look good.	4. Children should not have to earn their parents' love. Parents are supposed to love their children unconditionally.
5. Children are supposed to make their parents happy.	5. Children do not have the power to make their parents, or anybody else, happy any more than anyone else has the power to make them happy.
6. Children are supposed to please their parents, and if they work hard enough and are good enough, they will be able to please their parents.	6. Being pleased is a function of someone's personal value system. People are supposed to live to please God. This may or may not please their parents, too.

LIE	TRUTH
7. Children are supposed to meet all their parents' needs and give them a reason to feel good about themselves, that is, children should "fix" parents.	7. Children do not have the power to "fix" their parents or any other person. God doesn't send *children* to fix parents. He sent *Jesus* to do that!
8. All parents have accurately assessed each child's intrinsic worth and their treatment of each child is a statement about that child's true identity.	8. All human beings have intrinsic worth because each of us bears God's image. Therefore, all human beings deserve respectful treatment. Parents' treatment of their children is a statement about *the parents*, not about *the children*.
9. Loyal, loving, respectful children will always follow their parents' parenting rules, since their parents were perfect (or almost perfect).	9. Being a loyal, loving, respectful child does not mean pretending that either the parents or their rules are perfect. Loving and lying are not synonymous.

Which side of the chart sounds more correct and comfortable to you? If it's the left side, which I labeled as lies, the chances are you grew up in a fairly shame-bound family. That means you'll probably find changing your parenting patterns very difficult. I have a true story that explains why.

Our Parents' Brains or Our Own?

Meeting new brothers and sisters in God's family is one of the most delightful aspects of the traveling and speaking I do. One of these Christian brothers is a fortyish fellow I'll call "Byron." He's a committed Christian, a respected counselor, a dedicated husband, and dad to two sons. Byron also is the only offspring of a miserable union of an alcoholic father and a highly controlling mother.

Byron's dad died years ago. His mom lives several states away from her son and grandsons. (Byron assured me that's no accident. He worked it out that way.) Although he dreads it, once each year Byron packs up his wife and boys and treks to his mom's place for a visit. On last year's trip, the eight-and ten-year-old sons noticed Byron becoming more agitated as they got closer to Grandma's house. Byron explained it was not a relaxed, pleasant time for him since he had many sad memories about what happened in that house when he was a child.

The older boy asked for examples, and Byron carefully worded his response as he described his mother's attempts to control his every thought and action. When Byron finished, his ten-year-old son said, "So, let me get this straight. When you were a kid, *your mother was your brain!*"

That really says it for many of us, doesn't it? When we mistake staying parent-brained for being loyal, we may refuse to reexamine the parenting our parents modeled for us. So we'd likely live and parent on the Lies side of the chart.

That won't change until we give ourselves permission to develop our own brains by sifting through our beliefs about parent-child relationships to separate truth from lies. I did not say we should assume that everything we learned from our parents is a pack of lies. I know parents who operate by this parenting method. As one of them summarized it, "I ask myself what would my folks do in this situation, and then I do the exact opposite."

In contrast to this all-or-nothing thinking, our Heavenly Parent tells us in 1 Thessalonians 5:21 to examine all things carefully and hold on to only what is genuinely good, right, and true. Begin to experience the freedom inherent in this divine directive as it applies to your parenting. We can use our God-given brains and move into the healthier, more biblical concepts expressed on the right side of the chart. If we reclaim our brains and make that mental shift, we are well on our way to meeting the second major parenting challenge.

Major Challenge 2: Shifting Parenting Loyalties

Do you put more thought and emotional energy into being your parents' child or into being your child's parent? I wish someone had asked me this before Garth and I had our children. Since no one did, I had to stumble into this loyalty shift business on my own. And I bruised my kids as I stumbled.

I was raised believing that good mothers have daughters who play the piano. This was a law of the universe at least as immutable as some of the lesser laws, like gravity. Later as a parent, I knew my mother felt better when she saw me being a good mother by mothering the way she had. So naturally, I determined to please my mother and squeeze my daughter, Becky, into a musical mold.

Becky is a person of many talents and interests. So she wasn't thrilled with my push to make her put all her eggs into a Steinway basket. The harder I pushed, the more Becky hated the piano. I was totally clueless about why I had such a relentless compulsion to keep pushing. I simply believed I was doing what every good mother should do. Since I've published this story before, I'll just repeat it the way I told it in *Shame-Free Parenting*.

> I'm not exactly sure what happened. Maybe I finally heard Becky when she said, for the zillionth time, "Just because you loved to play the piano doesn't mean I have to—I'm not you!" (She understood more about individuality at eight than I did at thirty-three.) After Becky left for school that morning, I prayed and wept before the Lord about the entire situation.
>
> God reminded me of all the times my mother had conveyed that my piano recitals, radio program, and other musical activities were more about *her* being a "good mother" than they were about *me* using God-given ability. I saw too that I had believed Becky's musical performance was a commentary about *me* and my parenting abilities rather than a commentary about *her* and her musical abilities.
>
> As long as I held this "children exist to validate their parents" perspective, I *had* to make Becky keep taking piano lessons so that the world would know I was a good mother. It sounds very melodramatic . . . now, but that morning I took a momentous step in my life and my parenting. Perhaps for the first time, *I clearly understood the need to transfer my primary loyalty from being my parent's child to being my child's parent.*[2]

Before I began my purposeful loyalty shift I used Becky as a resource to gain my mother's approval. To one degree or another, we will all do that with our children until we make that essential mental shift from child-of-my-parent to parent-of-my-child. But we'll never shift our focus until we break out of our shame-based guilt and performance-focused lifestyles.

Changing Patterns of Performance-based Self-worth

When we believe the shame lie that says only perfect people deserve life and love, we'll likely experience existence guilt. When this is the case, we may unknowingly use our children as resources to validate our existence worthiness by expecting them to look perfect so we will look perfect. This replicates the core wounding mechanism our parents used with us.

We find evidence of this in the approaches we use to motivate our children. Our shame-based child motivation attitudes reflect our attitudes toward ourselves, which we learned, of course, from our parents' child motivation attitudes. What does this kind of parenting look like?

The following chart may help you recognize whether you view yourself and your children from a shame-based, performance-focused perspective.

Contrasting Self and Child Motivation Approaches[3]

HELPFUL ATTITUDES AND ACTIONS (See Self and Child as Human Beings)	HURTFUL ATTITUDES AND ACTIONS (See Self and Child as Human Beings)
I belong to God by creation (and if I have asked Jesus to be my Savior and Lord, by salvation), so my major task is to know and love God and seek to do His will for my life.	I belong to my parents and to others who need and care for me. My major task is to please and perform for them (as perfectly as possible) so they will approve of me so I can feel good about myself.
My child belongs to God, so my major task is to help my child be the person God created by teaching him/her to know and trust God.	My child belongs to me, so I have the right to press my child into the service of my shame-based perfectionistic needs.
I emphasize the internal perspective of developing my own and my child's character.	I emphasize an external perspective of promoting/polishing my own and my child's performance.
I take a long view for the purpose of character development, that is, I let my child learn the consequences of procrastination by getting a poor grade on a project done the night before it's due.	I take a short view for the appearance of perfect performance, that is, I do my child's project myself the night before it is due so that my child will maintain the highest possible grades.

HELPFUL ATTITUDES AND ACTIONS (See Self and Child as Human Beings)	HURTFUL ATTITUDES AND ACTIONS (See Self and Child as Human Beings)
I talk primarily about my child as an authentically struggling Christian, a very loving spouse, a tenderhearted boy or girl, a sincerely questioning teen, an honest employee, a wise parent, and/or a lover and student of God's Word.	I talk primarily about my child as the doctor, the ballet star, the select soccer hero, the youngest company vice-president in history, the pee-wee league all-star, or the winner of the Sunday school's Bible verse memorization contest.
I usually ask myself and my child: "Did you enjoy yourself, and/or learn anything?"	I usually ask myself and my child: "Did you win?" or "Were you the best?"
In myself and in my child, I affirm and reward brave attempts as well as obvious successes.	In myself and in my child, I affirm and reward winning only and believe that second place is no place!

Which style seemed more familiar? As we've seen already, we're likely to parent the way we were parented, which is probably just what our folks did. How else would we or they parent? So don't shame yourself for not automatically knowing how to be a consistently adequate, non-shaming parent. Just remember we can *learn* what we don't know. But we're not apt to risk learning healthier parenting techniques without first making the necessary loyalty shift we're examining here. If we fail to shift our primary focus from being a child to being a parent, we'll continue using our poor kids as crowbars!

Kids or Crowbars?

Some of us have been striving all our lives to figure out the combinations to our parents' hearts. Without realizing it many of us see our kids as human crowbars we can use to finally pry open the storehouse of our parents' approval which they have conditionally rationed or completely refused us so far.

This kids-as-crowbars mentality springs directly from our senses of shame. This is the logic: If I had been a better child, my parents would have been better parents. They never really loved and approved of me because I was not as good as other children. But my children are good and lovable enough to earn my parents' approval. If I keep urging my kids to do everything my parents wanted me to do and do it *perfectly*, maybe someday my parents will approve of me, too.

I've begun to suspect that despite all our best efforts and our obsessive attempts to use our children's best efforts, *some of us will never receive the treasured emotional nurturance we seek from our parents*. The treasure-house of our parents' nurturing love and approval may be empty, its precious treasure stolen years ago by those trust bandits who deeply wounded them.

Clearly most parents are not so deeply wounded and empty within. But if our parents are extremely hurtful people, we must ask ourselves this painful question: "If they were ever going to give me their loving acceptance and approval, wouldn't they have done it by now?" Think of how hard you've worked for it.

Isn't it time to begin accepting our parents as they are—as they really are? Only when we grieve the death of that dream which features June and Ward Cleaver act-alikes in the parenting roles can we reinvest all the energy we've spent trying to get what some parents can never give. Then we can use that energy to alter the course of our families' futures. And that's no small achievement.

Cycle Breakers and Cycle Makers

All of us must answer the same question our parents had to answer. Will we continue to run the assigned laps in our hurtful families' wretched relays of intergenerational pain— that ongoing cycle of hurting, hating, and hurting again? Or will we break that cycle and start a new cycle of healing and helping?

"I just wish I could start over with what I know now. I'd be a much better dad, if I could just start over again." That's how Jeremy expressed his frustration about not beginning his changing, healing process until his three children were young adults. I told him what I'm telling you and what I told myself: *We can* start over again, and again, and again.

We can't go back to that first step in our parenting paths. But we can start over right where we are. As Plutarch said, "My family history begins with me." That might seem like philosophical fantasy, considering the heavy influences of our ancestors. We can't change what's gone before us, and we certainly can't change our parents. Yet Plutarch is right. We do have the opportunity to profoundly alter what comes after us because *we can change our children's parents*. Our heavenly Parent is deeply committed to this parent-child issue. He intends parents' and children's hearts to be turned toward each other. (See Mal. 4:6.)

Finally, how do we cope with the pain of seeing that we've hurt our children? We must entrust them to the father-heart of God. He loves us and our children enough to let us all hurt so we can all learn for ourselves that only God can truly comfort and heal.

Specific Change Strategies

Since many of us do not so much undertake change as we wage all-out war, remember that there are no perfect parents. And you are unlikely to change *that*. I've learned by experience that when we manage to be consistently adequate our kids turn out wonderfully well.

1. *Learn as much as possible about healthy, biblically patterned parenting.* In addition to reading books, purposefully find some consistently adequate parents who model what you read.

2. *Tell your children that you intend to change your parenting practices.* In an age-appropriate manner, let your children know that you will be practicing new, healthier ways of relating to them. Tell them also that you know you won't ever be a perfect parent anymore than they will ever be perfect children.

3. *Get help to stop using your children to win approval from or keep peace with your parents.* Most of us do not suddenly get a light-bulb-turning-on kind of insight about this, and that's why we usually need help. This is absolutely crucial if we were physically or sexually abused by a parent, stepparent, grandparent, or others. Without realizing it, we could expose our children to dangerous situations with unsafe family members un-

less we experience substantial healing from such hands-on abuse.

4. *Lovingly launch your children on their own healing, changing journeys.* One of the brightest, bravest people I ever counseled came from an extremely religious but abusive home. She had a deep love for Christ, a seminary degree, and a broken heart. The longer we worked together in counseling, the more fully she realized how deeply she had wounded her three children with her violent anger.

As her personal healing progressed, she wanted to give her children something she had never received from her own parents—the purposeful permission to get help for healing her inner wounds. At my suggestion, she wrote the following letter which she plans to give to her three children when they are older.

My precious children,

I want you to know I have deep regrets and anguish for having been a dysfunctional parent to you. I have betrayed the innocent and absolute trust you had in me numerous times over the course of your young lives. Even though I have apologized to you and have expressed my remorse, I know extensive damage and brokenness has occurred within your emotions and spirits.

Tears well up in my eyes when in your sweet innocence you still tell me you love me. And you are just that—totally innocent. Nothing you did and nothing about you deserved the wounds you received from me. I am ashamed that I have caused you these horrible hurts and scars. My heart agonizes over the thoughts of the emotional surgeries you will each need to undergo and the processes you will go through to recover from the emotional damage.

As the injuries are opened and examined, you will have times when you will feel only anger and rage at me. It will not be easy for you or me to face such ugliness. But I want you to receive wise and skilled counsel and I want you to feel free to tell the truth—the horrible, painful truth. You don't need to protect me. Your healing and recovery are more important. I know you will never be able to fully forgive me, or fully get past these hurts, until you have thoroughly seen what it is you need to forgive and what needs to be healed.

I really do love you,

Mom

She told me that this letter "was very difficult to write, but it comes from the deepest parts of my heart." This is a clear example of how a parent's new, healthy choice to get help for herself frees her children to get help. This woman is determined that, with God's guidance and empowering, she will break the intergenerational cycle of abuse in her family.

So many of us would give almost anything to get a letter like this from a parent like this. We may never *have* parents like this, but by God's grace and our commitments to change, we can *be* parents like this.

Forgivers' H.O.P.E. Chart

KEY ISSUES	SEEING TRUTH	NEW CHOICES	NEW PRACTICING
Separating Parenting Lies from Truths	I've not ever purposefully evaluated my parenting beliefs	Separate the truth from the lies in my parenting beliefs	Consistently think and act on truth in my role as a parent
Shifting Primary Parenting Loyalty	I've been focused more on being my parents' child than my child's parent	Put more thought and energy into being my child's parent and less into being my parents' child	Consistently choose to be more invested in the role of my child's parent than in the role of my parents' child

---

Pause to Ponder and Pray

PONDER: Use the H.O.P.E. chart to find where you are in your changing and healing process in the area of parenting wounds.

✔ As you compare the lies and truths about parent-child relationships shown in the chart, where do you have the greatest struggle?

✔ How is that struggle manifested in your relationships with your children?

✔ What do you need to do to improve those relationships?

✔ Are you willing to do that?

✔ When will you begin?

PRAY: Lord, I confess that I often value my children most for what they do to make me look good. Please help me love and accept them for who they are—precious bearers of your image and priceless gifts from your hand. Amen.

Just Ahead

We've looked at *so* much hurt, wounding, and pain in so many areas of our lives. What do we do with this sense of utter personal brokenness? Is there truly hope for significant healing? Hope that hurt people can do more than hurt people?

We need some answers to these and other critical questions. They're coming next.

CHAPTER
Fifteen

Help for Hopeful
Tomorrows

I fully realize that I have not
succeeded in solving all of the issues.
Indeed, I know
I have not solved any of them completely.
And the solutions I have suggested
only lead to more problems
(some of which we weren't aware
were even issues when we began).
To sum it all up,
in some ways I know we are as confused as ever,
but I believe that we are confused
on a much higher level
and about far more important things!

I don't know who penned these words, but they capture my
thoughts as I begin this last chapter. Put differently, our

recovering processes resemble packaging a live octopus. Just about the time we think we've got it all wrapped up, something else pops out! That's why it's more realistic to say, "I'm committed to a changing process," rather than saying, "I'm completely changed."

Lifelong Changing

Some of us still wrestle with the concept that says change is the journey, not just the destination. Sometimes our steps are buoyant, bounding leaps. Other times our steps seem more like lead-footed shuffling or even about-to-crash stumbling. Most often, it's something in between. But as long as we're shuffling or stumbling in a new, healthier, more truth-led direction, we're in the process. Unfortunately many of us compare our stepping to others' stepping and worry that we aren't doing it right.

We need to let each of our change journeys develop as uniquely as we do. So many factors contribute: the depth of our wounds, the support and helping resources available to us, and the level of our cooperation with the Spirit of God, to name a few. God seems so much more realistic about all this than we are. (I suspect that's because he knows us perfectly, while we labor under delusions of being stronger or weaker than we really are.)

In Isaiah 40:31, God pictures three levels of functioning in his children. Some "soar on wings like eagles," others "run and [do] not grow weary," and still others "walk and [do] not . . . faint" (NIV). I've noticed lately that I have fewer fainting days, a lot more running days, and even more soul-stretching, soaring days than I used to have. But if I expected nothing but soaring, I'd be in big trouble, wouldn't I?

Have your soaring expectations crashed or sent you into a tailspin of disappointment? Please remember that God understands and accepts you even if you are barely managing to walk without fainting at this place in your lifelong healing process. When I contemplate a lifelong process, I need a steadying, strengthening hope to sustain me. I need it especially when I suspect that process holds the agony of defeat at least as often as the thrill of victory.

We Need Hope

What fuels our lifelong mending, healing, changing journeys? The life affirming nature planted within us by our living, life-giving God. God is committed to life from beginning to end:

- God is the birther when we "must be born again."

- God is the healer when we've been "wounded unto death."

- God is the grave robber when we've buried our futures and our hopes.

Our wise and loving God liberates our pain-entombed hope because he knows, far more than we, that without hope we die.

Hope for what? Certainly not for painless living. Let's imagine our childhood wounders come to us tomorrow to say, "Yes, I did it and I'm so sorry; please forgive me," and we do. Even then we are stuck with our characters and lives shaped by the wounds. And in our misguided efforts at self-supervised healing, we know we lay new wounds upon old—in ourselves and in others we love and never meant to hurt. No, it's not hope for pretending the wounds—those we've taken or given—never were.

And it's not even hope for complete erasure of our weakness and suffering. God has a plan for those products of our hurting and hurtful lives, even though we would just as soon have him remove all traces of our wounds.

Stewardship of Weakness

God calls us to be good stewards (that means, wise managers) of all his gifts and of our lives. God means all aspects of all of our lives, including the personal weaknesses caused, in part, by our childhood wounds. (Of course, many of our weaknesses are the result of our sin-flawed humanity.)

As I read my Bible I find verse after verse where God asks us to bring him our weakness so he can bear it with us. That's a far cry from what many of us think God wants to do with our weakness, isn't it? Especially if we were raised on the real-Christians-are-strong-all-the-time doctrine popular in some churches.

Actually, in Romans 8:26, Scripture tells us that God the Holy Spirit wants to help us "in our weaknesses," not berate us or take us out of our weakness, but help us. The word-picture in the Greek term translated *help* portrays someone, the Spirit of God in that specific verse, coming alongside us to help us bear our overburdening loads. As if that weren't hope-generating enough, there's more.

In 2 Corinthians 12:9 God promises to clearly display his universe-creating strength in our times of weakness. All that, and his pledge of sufficient grace at those times as well.

If we began to take seriously God's call to a stewardship of weakness, what would we learn? We'd experience the truth that God does not abandon us just when we need him most. Instead he wants us to let him come close beside us to help at our times of greatest weakness. And our fear of personal weakness would evaporate like morning fog in the bright promise of his strength and grace.

Weakness is one thing; suffering is another. And we may not be as sure that God can give anything good when we give him our suffering.

Stewardship of Suffering

I've noticed that, like aging, suffering does not necessarily improve people. It seems to make some folks better and others bitter. I don't think the difference is in the suffering; it's in the folks. More specifically, the difference is in what they do with the suffering.

Remember the beautiful sketch of Jesus comforting the wailing sufferer? If you don't, turn back to page 181 to refresh your memory. God longs for us to come to him with our sorrows and our suffering so that we'll know him as a comforter.

We hear a lot more about our Creator God than our Comforter God, don't we? But he is both. And most of us hurt people need to know a whole lot more about the comforting part of God's nature. Now it's one thing to hear about divine comfort and it's a quantum leap to experience it personally.

I have good news and bad news about experiencing God's comfort. The good news is: *We will really, truly experience God's comfort* when we suffer. God promises that and he does not lie. What's more, millions through the ages can testify to the reality of God's supernatural comfort. Count me among them.

The bad news is: We will really, truly experience God's comfort *when we suffer.* God's comfort is the greatest show on Earth. But sometimes the price of the ticket nearly kills you!

What greater display is there of God's many characteristics for his children stranded for a spell on this sin-sick sphere than his comfort? Since we are not stranded alone, God tells us to be conduits of his comfort. We drink in all we need, and still have an overflow to share with others. (See 2 Cor. 1:3–4.)

If God's comfort is so superabundantly available when we suffer with our painful wounds, does that mean he'll completely erase all the scars? I often get asked questions like that in conferences or counseling sessions. Sometimes they're phrased as, "Will I ever get over this?" I've learned from experience that when you and I ask questions like this, we're often seeking magic. We may want to hear that we can live and function just as though the hurt never happened.

But it did. And wounds leave scars. God factors even the scars into his divine equation.

Wearing the Scars of Hope

Our son, our daughter-in-law, and the world's most adorable grandchild live in Atlanta and attend First Baptist Church where Dr. Charles Stanley is senior pastor. When we visit that large church, I've noticed that a woman interprets the messages for deaf attenders. I watched her graceful gestures one Sunday, and wept when I realized the sign used for Jesus. In rapid succession, she touched the palms of her open hands—first left then right—with the middle finger of her gently curved opposite hand. The officially recognized sign for Jesus points to the marks of his death.

Do you see it too? As the songwriter says, Jesus is known by his scars! Ever since his cosmic Calvary wounding, his

death, and his rollicking resurrection, Jesus has been identified by his scars. Remember when he invited timid Thomas
to believe the scars when he couldn't believe the other
disciples' news of the resurrection?

To the hearing impaired and to all the rest of us, Jesus
comes wearing a signboard written on flesh, advertising
execution. But he comes with so much more. Jesus establishes his identity with his scars because *he is alive.* Execution scars on a corpse may tell us how that person died, but
they can't give us hope or tell us how to live. Jesus' scars
speak of triumph over betrayal. Victory over evil. Life after
death. Hope beyond despair.

As hurt people, we too wear scars. And God has a stewardship plan for our scars.

Stewardship of Scars

The subject of scars strikes close to home with me. You see
I form what is called keloid tissue when I receive cuts,
whether from carelessness or surgery. This means that instead of a nice little thin line from an incision, I have something that looks more like an unforgiving ridge of fleshy rope
still angry about being so ill-treated. Your scars might whis-
per. Mine shout.

That's what scars do. They speak, some loudly and others
softly. But they all have a history to tell. Good stewardship
of our scars involves letting them tell *his* story. I think that
letting our scars—the signs of our woundings—speak forth
God's story, describes what Scripture calls a "sacrifice of
praise."

I've heard a sacrifice described as giving up something we
can't do without. We can transfer that definition of a material sacrifice into the realm of language. So a spoken sacrifice
of praise means saying something we never could say. We
could never do it, that is, without God's supernatural scar-
transforming intervention.

Never in my wildest nightmares could I ever have imagined myself going around the country telling total strangers about the most painful experiences of my life—showing
them my scars, as it were. Even writing them down in black

and white, if you can believe it. I'm astounded time and again as I see God use the very things I grieved and regretted most. Those scars become not only a means to mold my character and to minister comfort to others, but they tell the story of God's life-transforming grace and death-transcending power.

The Greatest Hope

"Is that it? That's the best you have to offer in this 'hopeful tomorrow' chapter?" Some of you may be saying something like that to yourselves about now. I'll admit that lofty promises of total healing and painless futures would sell more books. I remember well buying quite a few based on titles that promised "victory" or "triumph" or "total" something or other that I longed to experience.

Many of us have gone through life looking for contentment in a person, a cause, a career, a marriage, a child, a church, or an endless list of other contentment containers. And, of course, we expected a lifetime guarantee.

Yet, here we are wounded and weary, our contentment containers long run dry. What a miserable, painful, exciting, hopeful place to be!

Only when we're at the end of ourselves will we reach for something beyond. Only when blinders of shame come off and Band-Aids of perfectionism break down, will we let God replace our unbearable yokes with his unbelievable grace.

Only then can God's love pour in. Of all hopes, this is the greatest—the promise of God's everlasting love.

He plasters that promise from one end of his Word to the other. Jesus was the consumate container—the incandescent explainer of God's everlasting love. Just think of how Christ's ministry matches our misery. We come bruised, broken, and bound. Jesus comes healing, mending, and releasing. At this perfect fit of need and provision, we see the union of God's scars and God's everlasting love.

Pause for a moment as you reflect on this lovely interpretation of that truth.

"I HAVE LOVED THEE WITH AN EVERLASTING LOVE ..." JER 31:3

Hopeful Tomorrows

God offers hope in as many forms as our hope-stealing pain.

- Hope for stewardship of weakness and suffering that brings good to us and others, while it brings glory to him.

- Hope that we will see more clearly how our wounding experiences fit into his whole design of our lives.

- Hope that as we embrace the reality of choice, change, and transformation, our scars will sing the praises of our living Savior.
- And hope that sees in the splintered fragments of our broken lives the reflection of his empty tomb.

Even hurting people need no more. Our loving God gives no less.

Appendix A:
Survivor Traits

Check the traits that (totally or partially) describe you and/or your past or current experiences.

__ 1. **Extreme and/or long lasting depression:** presence of clinical symptoms (including early morning waking, change in appetite, loss of energy, and diminished interest in usual activities); sometimes the depression is paralyzing; general sadness; crying "for no reason."

__ 2. **Helpless/hopeless feelings:** a "victim approach" to life with belief that "I can't change things/ things always turn out the same terrible way"; a general feeling of dissatisfaction with life—"nothing is working"; passivity; feeling like a child.

__ 3. **Addictive/compulsive disorders:** eating disorders (obesity, anorexia, bulimia); alcohol and/or drug addiction or abuse (or total abstinence unrelated to health or religious convictions).

__ 4. **Sleep disturbances:** fear of the dark; fear of sleeping alone; nightmares or night terrors, especially of threatening pursuit and/or entrapment.

__ 5. **Throat problems:** frequent, stress-related sore throats; swallowing and gagging sensitivity; suffocation feelings (including repugnance to water on face when bathing or swimming).

__ 6. **Alienation from your body:** not feeling "at home" in your own body; insensitivity to signals from your body; poor body care; poor and/or distorted body image.

__ 7. **Specific health problems:** stomachaches ("nervous" and/or "acid stomach"); colitis; spontaneous vaginal infections; unexplained pain in arms, legs, genitals and/or elsewhere.

__ 8. **Unusual clothing habits:** wearing a lot of clothing even in summer; preference for baggy clothes; resistance to removing clothing when bathing or swimming; sleeping fully clothed.

__ 9. **Self-mutilation:** cutting (skin carving); hitting; burning oneself.

__10. **Self-destructive thoughts/behaviors:** recurring suicidal thoughts and/or attempts; frequent self-injurious "accidents"; a "punishing" attitude toward yourself.

__11. **Sexual problems,** e.g., impersonal sex (promiscuity and/or prostitution); feeling "betrayed" by your body when experiencing sexual pleasure; strong aversion to (or need for) certain sexual acts; sexual avoidance and/or "response shutdown"; crying after orgasm; sexualizing of meaningful relationships; must be the sexual aggressor (or cannot be); sexual "acting out" to satisfy revenge needs; sexual arousal in response to abuse or anger; sexual fantasies of being dominated and/or raped; sexual identity problems.

__12. **Memory gaps**: ages five to eleven are "a total blank"; can remember what happened at school, etc., but can't remember anything about what went on inside your home; memory block(s) regarding certain person(s).

__13. **Nervousness about being watched or surprised**: extreme/exaggerated startle response as an adult; cowering in corners, hiding, and other security-seeking behaviors as a child.

__14. **Gender/race specific anger/hatred**: anger at/hatred of all males if perpetrator was a male; anger/hatred toward perpetrator's ethnic group/race.

__15. **Mistrusting your sanity and sense of reality**: feeling different and/or "crazy"; mistrusting your own perceptions/ observations; feeling you are "real" and everyone else is "unreal" (or vice versa); may include sensory distortions such as "tunnel vision."

__16. **Trust extremes**: inability to trust even when appropriate, or too much trusting too soon.

__17. **Fear of losing control**: obsession with power, control, territoriality; attempts to control things that don't matter just to feel a sense of control (obsessive/compulsive behaviors).

__18. **Abusive relationships**: a tendency to pick extremely disrespectful, abusive, and/or battering lovers/spouses/friends.

__19. **Difficulty concentrating and/or listening**: problems comprehending and need to reread material you are attempting to learn.

__20. **Drastic revenge fantasy**: formulating plans to expose, humiliate, punish perpetrator(s).

__21. **Emotional numbness**: a general "blah" feeling, numb emotional state; inability to identify the emotion(s) you are feeling.

__22. **Phobias**: claustrophobia (fear of cramped, enclosed places), agoraphobia (fear of experiencing panic/anxiety attacks while out in public), etc.

__23. **Self-hatred/shame**: feelings of contempt and self-loathing; feeling you are different and less valuable than other people; feeling like "damaged goods."

__24. **Use of fantasy**: frequent and/or long-term escapes into fantasy.

__25. **Touch aversion**: excessive dislike/fear of being touched (especially without warning).

__26. **Hypervigilance**: scanning your environment to ensure your safety; need to closely watch the significant people in your life; possessiveness; jealousy; intense fear of someone hurting your child.

__27. **Repressed tears or screams**: feeling like you want/need to scream and/or sob; hearing a child scream and/or sob inside your head.

__28. **Anger/rage extremes**: unreasonable and inappropriate outbursts of anger/rage; fear of actual or imagined rage; constant anger; inability to recognize, acknowledge, or express any anger.

__29. **Punishing attitude toward self and others**: unreasonable expectations; perfectionism.

__30. **Authority figure problems**: intense dislike and/or distrust of authority figures.

__31. **Spiritual problems**: unbiblical concepts of God as cruel, uncaring, etc.; problems trusting God; problems praying "Our Father."

__32. **Avoidance of mirrors**: as response to shame/low self-esteem/ poor body image issues.

__33. **Mental and/or verbal hypervigilance**: fear of expressing your thoughts/opinions; extreme care in monitoring your words; quiet-voiced, especially when needing to be heard.

__34. **Memory fragments and/or flashbacks**: sensory flashes experienced as an awareness or sense of a confusing, dangerous, painful, and/or threatening feeling and/or scene; frequently only the memory of what happened before the abuse and after the abuse is remembered at first.

__35. **Use of trance/depersonalization/dissociation**: disconnecting from the here-and-now, going numb, and/or into your "safe place" in a crisis/stressful situation associated with particular emotions (such as anger), memories (such as physical pain/sexual abuse), and/or situations (such as intercourse).

__36. **Extreme sensitivity to abandonment**: experiencing deep sadness/depression, fear, and/or anger when a friend/spouse forgets a social engagement or when a therapist goes on vacation.

__37. **Extreme sensitivity to needs/desires/emotions of others**: ability to "read" people accurately and to anti-cipate their wishes; instinctively knowing and doing what others want/need.

Often incest victims forget that the abuse ever occurred. However, the effects continue into adult life. If you "find yourself" on this list of survivor traits, you *could* be an incest survivor. Many of the traits are common to survivors of other types of child abuse too. However, *traits 5-14, 23-27, and 32-35 are particularly indic-*

ative of past sexual abuse. Finally, remember that no matter how ashamed you feel, please believe that you are not alone. Begin right this moment, my friend, telling yourself the truth about your abuse, namely:

"IT WAS NOT MY FAULT!"

Appendix B:
Discovering Your True Identity

These verses will help you see yourself as God sees you. Read them prayerfully as you ask God to reveal your true identity.

John 1:12; 1 Peter 2:9: I am God's child and I belong to Him.
Romans 8:35-39: Nothing can separate me from God's love.
Ephesians 1:4: I am chosen by God.
Ephesians 2:18; 3:12: I have access to God through Jesus.
Colossians 2:13-14: I am forgiven and my sin debt is paid.
Romans 8:1: I am not condemned.
Philippians 4:13: I am strengthened for all tasks to which God calls me.
1 Corinthians 6:19: My body is the Holy Spirit's abode.
Romans 5:1: I have peace with God through Jesus Christ.
Colossians 1:13: I have been rescued from the dominion of darkness and brought into the kingdom of God's Son.

Using your journal or a special notebook, write the verse, a personalized summary of the verse, and a past, present, or future application for it.

Your entries could follow this form:

> *And you, being dead in your trespasses and the uncircumcision of your flesh, He has made alive together with Him having forgiven you all trespasses, having wiped out the handwriting of requirements that was against us, which was contrary to us. And He has taken it out of the way, having nailed it to the cross* (Col. 2:13–14 NKJV).

Because I am forgiven of all my sins, I don't need to continue to punish myself for the abortion I had when I got pregnant in high school. God knows my heart, so he knows I have sincerely repented. That sin does not make me ineligible for God's gracious blessings.

Begin memorizing the verses that are most meaningful to you. Perhaps you can get together with other Christian friends to study and discuss these verses and others that tell you how God sees you. In your Christian bookstore you'll find Bible study guides available on this topic. I like *Self-Esteem: Seeing Ourselves as God Sees Us*, by Jack Kuhatschek, published by InterVarsity Press.

Appendix C:
Identifying Beliefs About Emotions[1]

SHAME-BOUND LIE	SHAME-FREE TRUTH
Emotions are unnecessary, bothersome, unspiritual, and embarrassing. I need to work on eliminating them.	Emotions are a gift from God and an integral part of our human natures which reflect his image. Jesus came to take away our sins, not our feelings!
Emotions are bad and dangerous, so it is safer when I avoid them.	Emotions are neither good nor bad. They can be expressed appropriately and I can learn to do that. I am less than the person God created me to be when I avoid feeling emotions.
If I begin to feel my emotions, I will "lose it," "fall apart," "go crazy," or hurt someone.	When I am able to feel my emotions, I become more authentic and alive. Recognizing and expressing emotions may feel strange and scary at first, but I can find "appropriate emoters" to help. I don't have to hurt anyone.
It is stupid to get all upset over things that happened years ago. It is best to "let sleeping dogs lie." Besides none of that affects me now.	It is appropriate for children to feel confused, afraid, sad, and/or angry when their parents neglect and/or abuse them. Those feelings did not go away just because I had to learn to disown them. They are still inside affecting my life today, and it is best to face them and feel them honestly.
When I felt sad as a child, no one was there for me. I couldn't stand to feel that despair and loneliness again. Besides, I am weak when I cry or act sad, and good Christians are never weak.	I have resources now as an adult that I did not have as a child. I can find more reliable (but imperfect) human comforters. And I know (or can know) God personally and have his comfort. Grieving childhood losses will be painful but I can survive it.
When I was a child, I was told I should never be angry. I just know God is angry about my anger, both my anger about the past and about present situations. Besides, good Christians never feel angry.	It is appropriate to feel angry about what angers God. Misleading and/or abusing children angers God. I can learn to express anger appropriately and without sinning (see Eph. 4:26).

Appendix D:
Representative Biblical Principles of Relating

List biblical principles for relating in your personal journal and describe their applications in your life. Here are a few examples:

"When Jesus saw him lying there and learned that he had been in this condition for a long time, he asked him, 'Do you want to get well?' " (John 5:6 NIV).

Principle: Jesus didn't invade a needy man's personal boundaries.

Personal Application Example: When I'm helping people, I need to respect them and their personal boundaries enough to ask them what they want me to do for them.

"Then because so many people were coming and going that they did not even have a chance to eat, [Jesus] said to them, 'Come with me by yourselves to a quiet place and get some rest' " (Mark 6:31 NIV).

Principle: Jesus encourages people-helpers to take care of themselves.

Personal Application Example: It's really all right for me to say no sometimes when I'm too exhausted to accept a task someone asks me to take—even at church.

"Jesus said, 'Let the little children come to me, and do not forbid them' " (Matt. 19:14 NKJV).

Principle: Jesus didn't let people tell him what to do, that is, he didn't allow them to send children away.

Personal Application Example: It's okay when I hold my own opinions, even when others disagree. I don't have to hide my views or values to be congenial or kind.

"If it is possible, as much as depends on you, live peaceably with all men" (Rom. 12:18 NKJV).

Principle: We should aim for peaceful relationships. But the phrase, "As much as depends on you," recognizes the truth that we can't control others' choices.

Personal Application Example: I want peace with my boyfriend, but I can't control his choices even when I violate my standards by doing that.

Appendix E:
Some Attributes of God[1]

God is compassionate as demonstrated in his mercy and loving kindness. ("The Lord is compassionate and gracious, slow to anger, abounding in love." Ps. 103:8 NIV)

God is forgiving because of his grace and mercy. Jesus paid our sin debts so that God could forgive sin while remaining holy and just. ("In him [Christ] we have redemption through his blood, the forgiveness of sins, in accordance with the riches of God's grace." Eph. 1:7 NIV. See also Rom. 3:23–26.)

God is immutable, i.e., he never changes. ("Jesus Christ is the same yesterday and today and forever." Heb. 13:8 NIV)

God is just because he always acts fairly, in accordance with his nature. ("He is the Rock, his works are perfect, and all his ways are just. A faithful God who does no wrong, upright and just is he." Deut. 32:4 NIV)

God is loving because of his nature and not because of anything we do to elicit his love. His love is expressed in actions toward us. ("God is love." 1 John 4:16 NIV)

God is omnipotent because he has unlimited power and ability. ("You have made the heavens and the earth by your great power and outstretched arm. Nothing is too hard for you." Jer. 32:17 NIV)

God is omnipresent because he is present everywhere in the universe at the same time. God is never "absent." ("'Am I only a God nearby,' declares the Lord, 'and not a God far away? Can anyone hide in secret places so that I cannot see him?' declares the Lord. 'Do not I fill heaven and earth?' declares the Lord." Jer. 23:23–24 NIV)

God is omniscient because of his unlimited knowledge and wisdom. ("You know when I sit and when I rise; you perceive my thoughts from afar. You discern my going out and my lying down; you are familiar with all my ways. Before a word is on my tongue you know it completely, O Lord." Ps. 139:2–4 NIV)

God is righteous because he only does what is right and is free from any wrong doing. ("The Lord is righteous in all his ways and loving toward all he has made." Ps. 145:17 NIV)

God is sovereign because he rules supremely over all creation. ("He does as he pleases with the powers of heaven and the peoples of the earth. No one can hold back his hand or say to him: 'What have you done?' " Dan. 4:35b NIV)

Appendix F:
Shame-Based Vs. Grace-Based Church Families[1]

SHAME-FULL CHURCH FAMILY Some-Grace Theology	GRACE-FULL CHURCH FAMILY All-Grace Theology
God is presented as a demanding Pharisee/Shepherd who drives his sheep.	God is presented as an understanding Father/Shepherd who leads his sheep.
Once, by God's grace, we trust in Jesus' righteousness to pay for our sins, God's acceptance is earned by performing and pleasing with our own good works and law-keeping.	From beginning to end, God's acceptance is solely the gift of his grace which we receive by trusting in Jesus' perfect work of fulfilling the law and dying to pay the penalty for our sins.
I am expected to be totally (or almost) transformed the moment I trust Christ.	I am expected to keep on being transformed by having my mind renewed as long as I live.
Since I should be totally transformed, i.e., perfect, I am a different-and-worthless Christian because I'm not perfect.	Since I am in a lifelong process of being transformed to be like Jesus, my imperfections don't surprise either me or God.
Members with obvious problems are an embarrassment to our church. Since *real* Christians have no serious problems, we don't need to bother making any provisions to help.	Members with obvious problems are expected since the past and present effects of sin in Christians' lives can cause serious problems. There are programs in place to provide appropriate help.
Small group Bible studies are dangerous places because someone might get close enough to see behind my mask of perfection and know I have problems.	Small group Bible studies are safe places to practice being maskless and real with others who do the same. It's great to go where I don't have to hide my problems.
Emphasis is on looking religious by wearing the right clothes and carrying the right translation of the Bible.	Emphasis is on developing a deeper relationship of love and trusting obedience with the Lord Jesus Christ.
Emphasis is on revealing and rebuking sinners.	Emphasis is on restoring repentant sinners.
Attendance at church activities is used as the main indicator of a person's true spirituality.	Acknowledges that true spirituality is reflected in total lifestyle and known only to God.

NOTES

Introduction

1. Barbara Bonner, "Adolescent Perpetrators," *APSAC Advisor*, Fall 1991, 13-14.

Chapter 1. The Problem of Unseen Wounds

1. Jesus "rejoiced greatly" at the good report of the seventy he had sent out (Luke 10:21) and wept at Lazarus' grave (John 11:35). Jesus also "deeply grieved" in Gethsemane (Matt. 26:38) and felt intense anger (John 2:14–16). And Jesus loved. He loved his disciples. He loved Lazarus and his sisters, who returned the affection, and he loved the "rich young ruler," who did not.
2. To learn more than you may have ever wanted to know about shame, its origins, effects, and solutions, see my book *Released from Shame* (InterVarsity Press, 1990).

Chapter 2. The Power of Unseen Wounds

1. Francis Brown, S. R. Driver, and Charles Briggs, *A Hebrew and English Lexicon of the Old Testament* (Oxford: Clarendon Press, 1968), 457.
2. Wilson, *Released from Shame*, 89.
3. J. S. Milner, K. R. Robertson, and D. L. Rogers, "Childhood History of Abuse and Adult Abuse Potential," *Journal of Family Violence* 5 (1990), 15–34.
4. Some translations use the word "wicked" (King James) or "offensive" (New International) instead of "hurtful" as the New American Standard does. All three translations describe a manner of living that is potentially harmful to oneself and to others.

Chapter 3. Hurt by the Unprepared and Unavailable

1. This description of biological shame is adapted from *Released from Shame*, 26-27.
2. The Associated Press, "Study: Scars from Abuse Can Last a Lifetime," *Cincinnati Enquirer*, February 18, 1991, A-8. Italics added.

Chapter 4. Hurt by Liars and Thieves

1. John Friel and Linda Friel, *Adult Children: The Secrets of Dysfunctional Families* (Deerfield Beach, FL: Health Communications, 1988), 35-36.
2. Gail Buchather, "The Circus Taught Him Love," *Parade Magazine*, August 18, 1991, 18-19.

3. The Associated Press, "Clown Draws 10-Year Sentence," *Cincinnati Enquirer*, December 15, 1991, D-2.

Chapter 6. Hurt by Childhood Choices

1. Walter Bauer, William Arndt, and F. Wilbur Gingrich, *A Greek-English Lexicon of the New Testament*, 2nd ed. (Chicago: University of Chicago Press, 1979), 752.

Chapter 7. Help for Healing Our Hurts

1. Ernie Larsen, *What I Practice, I Become* (St. Paul, MN: International Marriage Encounter, 1986), 17.
2. David Seamands, *Putting Away Childish Things* (Wheaton, IL: Victor Books, 1982), Preface.
3. Bauer, Arndt, and Gingrich, 417.
4. In a *Cincinnati Enquirer* (August 18, 1989, B-10) article, entitled "Toxic Parents Can Poison Children," reporter Terry Lawhead quotes the author of *Toxic Parents* as saying that therapist authors who encourage people to forgive their parents are writing "wimp books."

Chapter 8. Help for Healing Self-inflicted Wounds

1. Karen Peterson, "Behaviors Analyzed at Psychologists' Convention," *USA Today*, August 19, 1992, 5D.
2. Jeff and his delightful wife, Holly, live in Crystal, Minnesota, where Jeff is the Executive Director of Damascus, Inc., and the counseling pastor at Church of the Open Door. He writes about shame in his fine book *Tired of Trying to Measure Up* (Minneapolis: Bethany House Publishers, 1990).

Chapter 9. Help for Healing Friends and Spouses

1. The Associated Press, "Assault in Adolescence Leads to Higher Risk of Rape," *Cincinnati Enquirer*, August 17, 1992, A-3.
2. Scripture declares that all human hearts are "deceitful above all things," and this means that any person's deceitful heart has the potential for enormous evil. (See Jer. 17:9.)
3. This chart is adapted from one that first appeared in *Released from Shame*, 136.
4. This chart first appeared in *Released from Shame*, 139.
5. Melody Beattie, *Codependent No More* (San Francisco: Hazelden, 1987).
6. The Associated Press, "Living Together Risks Love," *Cincinnati Enquirer*, September 3, 1992, A-7.
7. Every time I give principles for healthy relationships I include Share-Check-Share because I think it's so valuable. I first discovered it in Herbert Gravits and Julie Bowden's

Guide to Recovery: A Book for Adult Children of Alcoholics
(Holmes Beach, FL: Learning Publications, 1985), 73.

Chapter 10. Help for Healing Leaders

1. Most of the material about employment-home conflict is taken from Tom's unpublished doctoral dissertation for the Union Institute. I had the delightful privilege of serving on Tom's doctoral committee.

2. Julia Duin, "Renewal Leader Pulkingham Admits Guilt," *Christianity Today*, September 14, 1992, 78.

3. David Johnson and Jeff VanVonderen, *The Subtle Power of Spiritual Abuse* (Minneapolis, MN: Bethany House, 1991), 103.

4. J. I. Packer, *Rediscovering Holiness* (Servant, 1992).

5. I heard Dr. Hart say this at the consultation on "Pastors in Crisis."

Chapter 11. Help for Healing Followers

1. Susan Hogan-Albach, "Pastors Struggle to Draw Relationship Boundaries," *Cincinnati Enquirer*, September 9, 1992, D-5.

2. "The Porn King Gets Off," *Time*, November 4, 1991, 37.

3. Jeff VanVonderen, *Tired of Trying to Measure Up* (Minneapolis: Bethany House Publishers, 1989), 71.

Chapter 12. Help For Healing Worshipers

1. *Cincinnati Enquirer*, August 25, 1992, East Central Extra, 2

2. This exercise first appeared in Chapter 6 of my book *Shame-Free Parenting* (InterVarsity Press, 1992). I am indebted to my senior pastor at Faith Evangelical Free Church in Milford, OH, Dr. Ray Dupont, for suggesting it.

3. Ann Trebbe, "Charting a '90s Path to Self-Help," *USA Today*, June 20, 1991, 1D. This quote and the briefer one after the next paragraph are taken from a "sidebar," titled "The 'Course' Curriculum," which appeared alongside the main article. The italics do not appear in the original.

Chapter 13. Help for Healing Forgivers

1. Michelle Lewis Starr, "A Terrible Thing to Waste," *Confident Living*, April 1991, 46-47.

2. Colin Brown, ed., *The New International Dictionary of New Testament Theology*, Vol. I (Grand Rapids: Zondervan, 1986), 697.

3. Arnold Fox and Barry Fox, "The Gift of Forgiveness: Giving Up the Emotional Toxins," *Changes*, May-June 1989, 18.

4. Now and then I write some poetry. "Release the Prisoner" is a recent effort.

Chapter 14.   Help for Healing Parents

1. *Shame-free Parenting*, 41.
2. *Shame-free Parenting*, 104–5.
3. *Shame-free Parenting*, 118.

Appendix C:

1. This chart is an adaptation of one that first appeared on page 121 in my second book, *Released from Shame*.

Appendix E:

1. *Released from Shame*, 195-196.

Appendix F:

1. This chart is an adaptation of one that first appeared on page 159 in *Released from Shame*.

248-WIL

Wilson, Sandra D.
Hurt People Hurt People

ISSUED TO

248·WIL

Wilson, Sandra D.
Hurt People Hurt People